STUDENT'S HARMONY BOOK

by

Preston Ware Orem

Price $1.50

CLAYTON F. SUMMY CO.
Chicago   New York
Printed in U.S.A.

Copyright, 1934, by Clayton F. Summy Co.
International Copyright

FOREWORD

It seems to have been the idea of the older theorists to make the study of harmony as complicated as possible: to befog the issue in the minds of those embarking upon the study of creative music so as to preclude the possibility of eventual success for the many. One has only to read some of the old books to realize just what was going on. Nevertheless, some of these old fellows had a wonderful command of matters theoretical, from their own standpoints. They just wanted it all for themselves.

Nowadays, time's pendulum seems to have swung in the other direction; we are all striving to make our subject as simple and as easy to understand as possible. So far, so good! But, are we not in possible danger of going too far in this present direction? For the last fifty years or so, most conservatories have insisted upon the attendance at the weekly Harmony Class of all vocal and instrumental students. At the best this attendance was but perfunctory; since only the really bright or exceptionally earnest students actually profited much. In more recent years the tendency has been to combine a certain amount of elementary harmony teaching with all instrumental work, particularly in piano teaching, where, naturally it belongs. This is due chiefly to the growth of public appreciation of the fact that music has become an integral part of general education. Hence it must be handled differently. Once upon a time piano playing was taught as a polite accomplishment; and, unquestionably we did make some good players, many of whom remained without much, if any, theoretical knowledge. Today we are striving both to make more players and, at the same time to develop a knowledge of the making of music and a love for the art of music itself.

But, here let us sound a warning. Let us preserve a proper balance. While we are theorising about music, let us, at the same time learn to play. Let us give plenty of time to our theoretical studies. Let us do them unhurriedly and with thoroughness. But, above all things, learn to play; make music heard. Harmony is something vital; it must be heard. There is much music on paper, written and in print, that looks a lot better than it sounds. We do not want that sort of thing.

The recent and very successful movement in favor of Group Musical Instruction has brought about many very desirable changes and improvements in teaching methods. It has served to popularize music instruction generally, and, in the elementary grades, to turn what used to be more or less of a task with younger students into a positive pleasure. Now, what has Harmony to do with all this? Much! In Piano Class Instruction particularly, there is manifested a very decided tendency to introduce certain Harmonic principles almost from the beginning. Very good! We have no objection. Rather, must we, when it comes to straight Harmony teaching, so plan our course as to assimilate and to build upon all that has been attained previously, and to observe closely the methods by which it has been accomplished. Such is the object of this book.

THE COMMON SENSE OF HARMONY

Common sense, more than anything else, is required in the study of any Art. If we can get at the root of the matter at once, so much the better.

In the study of this book, one thing after another must be mastered, in close succession; but nothing preceding may be left undone while the next subject is being approached.

Based upon the assumption that nothing is so well settled in the mind as by the actual writing of it, it is urged that even the musical examples be copied off elsewhere, after each new lesson. In the preparation of each new lesson, all Exercises to be done by the student should be tried out elsewhere before being placed in the Book. No one should attempt to write before the principle of the task assigned is thoroughly understood. An inexpensive Music Writing Book will be found handy for trying out all preliminary problems; serving also as a permanent record of one's work.

In attacking this book, the student must realize that he is right down to fighting weight. In the book itself, all is told as plainly as possible; and in as few words. There is no attempt at "fine writing" and no frills or complications. At the same time, our subject is a live one: we are preparing to make real Music. Consequently, we must feel the joy of it all; developing at the same time a sense of the aesthetic and of the picturesque.

What is expected of the student finally, so far as the study of this book is concerned, is: that he will know fully and freely the Scales; the Intervals; *all* of the Chords, together with their Cadences and Progressions; and be equipped with a full knowledge of the use and meaning of Tonality.

Preston Ware Orem

CONTENTS

	Page
Foreword	3
The Common Sense of Harmony	4

Lesson Number		Page
1	The Approach	7
2	The Attack	8
3	Progress	10
4	About the Scales	14
5	About the Intervals	18
6	More about the Intervals	21
7	Something about Triads	24
8	Triads and Intervals	26
9	More about Triads	30
10	About Common Chords	32
11	Making Some Use of the Common Chords	36
12	Setting Chords to a Melody	41
13	More about Melodies and Chords	45
14	About Inversions	47
15	More about the First Inversion	52
16	About the Second Inversion	54
17	About Numerals and Figures and their Application	57
18	More about the Second Inversion	61
19	About the Minor Scale	64
20	Using Minor Harmonies	68
21	All the Intervals	72
22	Beginning the Dominant Seventh Chord	75
23	Making Use of the Dominant Seventh Chord	79
24	Further Adventures with the Dominant Seventh	81
25	Back to the Minor	85
26	An Adventure into Tonality	91
27	Further Adventures	97
28	About Ninths	101
29	More about Ninths, and Some Other Matters	104
30	About Diminished Sevenths	108
31	About Elevenths and Thirteenths	114
32	About the Augmented Sixth, and Some Other Chords	120
33	Concluding	127

LESSON ONE
THE APPROACH

How shall we start? Let us first take account of stock; and then, set our stage.

How much do we already know? We may take it for granted that those who are beginning this book are familiar at least with the elements of notation: the Great Staff; note names in the G Clef and in the F Clef; note values; the Piano Keyboard and its geography. Many of us will know much more than this, but a review of this knowledge will not come amiss; it is possible, also, that certain readjustments will have to be made in order to promote a better understanding of certain matters as we go along. We are going to study Harmony now. The real thing. But let us approach it joyfully and with an enhanced interest. The things that will have been learned in school, in group instruction, in piano classes, in sight-singing will all prove helpful and contributory, after we have gathered them all into a general consensus of opinion.

The successful study of Harmony depends absolutely upon a mastery of each successive step, in proceeding from the known to the unknown. One limping step throws the whole mental process out of gear. Harmony is not a series of definitions, rules and principles to be learned by rote. It is rather the actual foundation of creative musical art.

Now, let us start with the assumptions that the word **Tone** means any musical sound; that musical sounds are the product of regular **Vibrations** of the air, or sound waves; that any given Tone has **Pitch** (highness or lowness), due to the relative intensity of its sound waves. With **Noise,** the product of irregular vibration, we are not concerned.

When we start to combine Tones and to sound them together we have begun the study of **Harmony.**

Now, some are going to say, "Well! why not begin?" "Why waste time over the things we already know?" Ah! Do you really know? How many actually know what Pitch is? How many of you have spoken of "playing a note," or have heard this expression, instead of the proper expression, "sounding a tone?" How many understand Vibration?

All probably have had some Ear-Training. Have some more at once. Experiment at the piano by seeing how strings are set into motion at the touch of the felt-tipped hammers and notice the ensuing Vibrations; oscillatory (back and forth) Vibrations, by-the-way. Experiment with other instruments, and endeavor to discover how Vibration is started in each. Strike inanimate objects one against another, and create Noise. Not too much of this latter. And, above all things, learn to think!

QUIZ No. 1

1. Upon what does the Study of Harmony depend for its success?
2. What is meant by the word Tone?
3. What is meant by Pitch?
4. From what does Noise result?
5. What is Harmony?
6. What causes Sound?

LESSON TWO
THE ATTACK

Once upon a time—in an old-established Eastern conservatory, the usual annual beginners' Harmony Class was started; made up of over fifty members; mostly girls, but including three or four men and a small boy. The class was supposed to last from October to June. It started out with flying colors, but the very first lesson assignment was a facer; all the Scales, Intervals and Common Chords. Naturally some members of the class knew something of all of these subjects, but their combined knowledge was surprisingly small. At the end of the season there remained in this particular class just four of the original members; three big girls and the aforesaid small boy. The three girls, who had memorized carefully all the Rules and practically everything else that was said to them, came through their written examinations with flying colors, but not one of them could harmonize satisfactorily a given melody, or even a given bass. The small boy, who had insisted upon a mastery of Principles rather than the written word, had made some real progress after an uphill struggle. While this may have been an extreme case, the experience as a whole was not unlike that of many classes of which we have known through the years.

This reminds us, that while we started something in Lesson One, we have not as yet really started Lesson Two. Let's begin! Of the headings mentioned above we will select the **Scales**. Who knows anything about Scales? Why and wherefore? In the Victorian Era, Scales were something that one practiced in order to be able to ripple up and down the Piano Keyboard in the fashionable drawing-room pieces of the day. Nowadays some seem to prefer tramping on the Keyboard with both feet. Or, is it both fists? In the study of Harmony we employ the Scales for certain definite purposes.

In dealing with the Scale, as in all other subjects dealt with in this book, we must insist upon plain thinking and plain talking. All must be direct and in logical sequence. We must throw away our musical crutches of all kinds. We have spoken of a Tone as a musical sound. In Harmony it is just that, and nothing else. It stands to reason, that, if music is made up of Tones of varying degrees of Pitch, we must have some method of assembling those Tones in a regular order. For this purpose the **Scale** or **Tone-Ladder** has been devised. There have been many forms of Scales; there may be many more in the future. Who knows? But, the Scale with which we have to deal chiefly in the study of Harmony is known as the **Major Scale**. The word Major means, as usual: Greater.

Now, in the making of music, Twelve Tones are employed. In the arrangement of these tones into various devices, Harmony is concerned chiefly. The Scale, especially the Major Scale, is the most logical starting point. We have spoken of differences in Pitch. The most minute difference in Pitch that may be found upon the Keyboard of the Pianoforte or upon most keyed instruments is known as a **Half-Step**. Now comes the disturbance! O all ye students, we do indeed know about the **Semi-Tone**; but for Harmony's sake let us abandon the expression here. If we are to speak of a Tone as a musical sound, then, a Semi-Tone is half a musical sound. How could it be done? The terms **Step** and **Half-Step** are safer.

It may be asked, "Can we not make a Quarter-Step?" Yes, indeed! Vocalists often make them, unconsciously. Players of stringed instruments, also, are apt to

THE ATTACK

produce them when their left hands are not properly "set" in the beginning. There are also some instruments to be found purposely tuned in this manner. When we consider, that, in the course of an evening's program by a concert band the pitch of the instruments may vary nearly as much as a Half-Step, these inventions may appear to be of little practical value.

To return to the **Half-Step.** Twelve separate Tones are used in the making of Music. Take, as a familiar illustration, the Keyboard of the Piano or the Organ; from any Piano Key to the next adjacent Key (black or white, as the case may be) is a Half-Step. From any Piano Key to the next Key but one (black or white) is a Whole-Step. Probably, all of you have had this before. But, fight it out to a finish, here and now. It is not sufficient to pick out Piano Keys and to look at the Keyboard. One must learn to hear these things. Play and sing Half-Steps and Steps until each may be recognized freely when heard and until either may be sung readily from any given starting Tone. This is the real beginning of Ear-Training. Let us in this exercise dispense with all Syllables, Numbers and Letter-Names. Use unnamed Tones until these measurements are established definitely, both mentally and orally. It will develop in a lesson or so, why it is so necessary to be so particular at this point. Our idea is to develop a knowledge of Harmony from the ground-floor. Let the teacher test out members of the class; and members of the class, one another.

QUIZ No. 2

1. What is the most minute difference in Pitch in common use?
2. What is a Scale?
3. What is the important Scale in Harmony?
4. How many separate Tones are used in making Music?
5. What is a Whole-Step?

LESSON THREE
PROGRESS

To return to that **Major Scale**. Many students seem to have placed the "cart before the horse," in this connection. In our anxiety to demonstrate clearly the difference between the Step and the Half-Step, we teachers may have unintentionally exalted the importance of the Scale. So many clever devices have been invented for helping students in this regard. The point is, however, that the Scale has grown out of the necessities of Creative Music: not Music from the Scales. Few of us can have escaped hearing the expression "Whole-Tone Scale," a rather meaningless expression applied to a form of Scale made up entirely of Whole-Steps. We mention this here because, in contrast, our Major Scale is not made up entirely of Whole-Steps, but of Whole-Steps and Half-Steps in a certain regular order and proportion: made up thus because our present tonal system demands it, and for no other reason.

Now come some expressions which we must all understand and upon which we must agree before going on further. All know, by now, that the first seven letters of the alphabet, A, B, C, D, E, F, G, are used in naming the Notes which we apply, respectively, to the various Tones, for purposes of distinguishing Pitch. When we proceed, letter by letter, from one letter to the next in order, we are proceeding by **Degrees** hence, a **Degree** may be either a Step or a Half-Step. The adjective that we apply to this process is the word **Diatonic** (meaning literally, through the tones): actually, from one Tone to the next, letter by letter, without any particular reference as to the placing of Steps or Half-Steps. At this stage, we are just clearing the way. Harmony study depends for its ultimate success upon absolute mastery of progressive steps.

The **Major Scale** consists of eight Degrees, arranged in a certain definite design of Steps and Half-Steps. It is made up of two equal portions of four Degrees each. These latter are known as **Tetrachords**. Each Tetrachord is arranged as follows: from the first degree to the second degree is a Whole-Step; from the second degree to the third degree is a Whole-Step; from the third degree to the fourth degree is a Half-Step. Let us construct our first Tetrachord. We will begin on our old friend "Middle C." Many may think "Why must we do this all over again?" Pray be patient! We are dealing now with music in the abstract and we are removing some crutches and other helpful devices, admirable as they may have been in the past. Here we are:

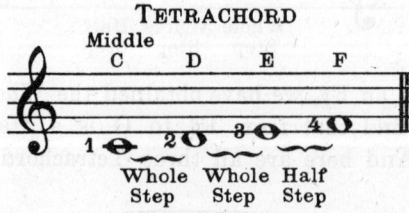

Let us analyze: from C to D is a Whole-Step. How do you know? Your ears should tell you by now. You can count the Piano Keys: there is a Black Key between the White Keys C and D. In addition one must learn to recognize Steps and Half-Steps on the Staff. This will develop as we go on. Next: from D to E is a Whole-Step (with the same reasoning as for the preceding). And again: from

E to F is a Half-Step. Why? The ears should be the best judge: besides, there is no Piano Key between the Keys for E and F. Just remember this first place on the Staff where you can find a Half-Step. Then the eye and the ear will both be satisfied. Piano students must remember that we may be dealing in the Harmony Class with Vocalists and Violinists and other Instrumentalists, also. No, we will not bother with Syllables! No make-shifts in Harmony! Now we can go on and build our second Tetrachord, thus completing the Major Scale. No apology is offered for our apparent slowness of approach. We are attempting to establish an exact mental attitude; for reasons which will appear later. To return: leaving a Whole-Step between the two Tetrachords, we have:

At last! Of course, you all know the Major Scale when you hear it. But please hear it better than ever; and hear it understandingly.

Now, let us see what will happen if we add still another Tetrachord to the two that we already have. We ended our second Tetrachord on C. Leaving a Whole-Step starts our third Tetrachord on D. If we proceed by Degrees (Diatonically), this is what we will get:

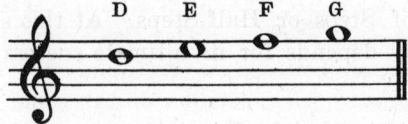

What is wrong with this? From D to E is a Whole-Step, but, from E to F is a Half-Step. Let the ear verify this. We must get another Half-Step. We will find it in the Black Key adjoining F. We will call this F♯, because we have **raised** or **Sharpened** the F. Bear in mind, we can never change the letter. We are proceeding by Degrees always.

Now, let us see and hear:

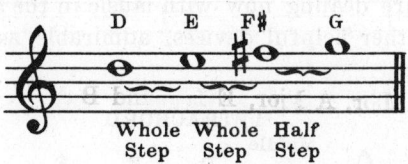

By changing the F to an F♯, we have obtained the Whole-Step where we wanted it, and, in addition, we find that from F♯ to G is a Half-Step, and all is well. Sing, play and think. And here are all three Tetrachords in order:

It will be observed, that, through the addition of another Tetrachord, we have also completed a new Scale. From C to C (the first two Tetrachords) we have one complete Major Scale; from G to G (second and third Tetrachords) we have another complete Major Scale.

As Tetrachord after Tetrachord is added the Scales will be found to overlap in this manner throughout. The second Tetrachord of each Scale becomes the first Tetrachord of each following Scale. Let us write out one more Tetrachord in the series. Proceeding by Degrees will give us:

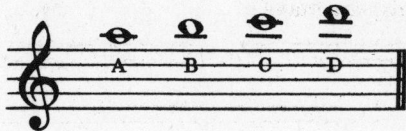

We find a Whole-Step between A and B, but a Half-Step only between B and C: So we must have recourse to C♯ to help us out. Then, from C♯ to D is a Half-Step; and, once more, all is well:

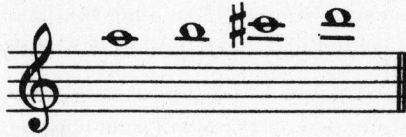

To return to our first Scale beginning on "Middle C": we note that this Scale begins on C and ends on C; hence its official title is: **The C Major Scale.** Having used eight White Keys to complete our Major Scale, and eight Degrees in which to write it, let us call the distance between its first and last Tones an **Octave**. It is always thus from any Tone to the repetition of the same above or below.

What Scale did we form by the addition of a third Tetrachord? The G Major Scale. And what did that last Tetrachord give us? The D Major Scale. One cannot make too much Eye and Ear training of all this.

Now, write: Tetrachords beginning on A, E, B, F♯; in the spaces indicated:

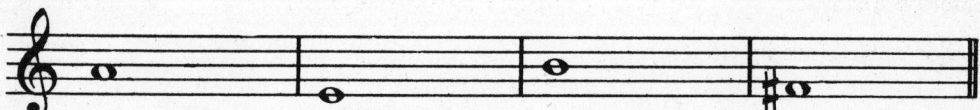

Next, write in full the D Major, A Major, E Major and B Major Scales. Play and sing them.

QUIZ No. 3

1. What is meant by a "Whole-Tone" Scale?
2. What is meant by a Degree?
3. What is meant by the word Diatonic?
4. Describe the formation of the Major Scale.
5. What is a Tetrachord?
6. Write (or recite) Tetrachords beginning on: D, F♯, G♯, D♭, A♭, G♭.

LESSON FOUR
ABOUT THE SCALES

Let us try another experiment. We will write the F Major Scale. At first, according to Degrees. In scale writing we must not write two notes in succession on the same Degree; nor must we skip a Degree. Here we are:

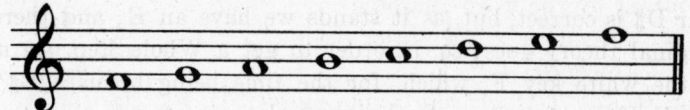

Let us see what fixing this one will need. From F to G is a Whole-Step; from G to A is a Whole-Step; **but,** from A to B, as it stands, is also a Whole-Step. We need a Half-Step. We have a sign which **sharpens** or raises a note; we have also a sign which **flattens** or lowers a note. Let us lower the B by placing a **Flat** before it. Then we have: A to B♭, a Half-Step. Thus:

THE F MAJOR SCALE

Correct! We know all about that second Tetrachord. It is the first that we learned.

From this constant overlapping of Tetrachords, with its constant linking together of Scales, we deduce the Principle, that: Scales having Tetrachords in common are called **Related Scales.** As an example: the second Tetrachord in the Scale of F Major is the first Tetrachord in the Scale of C Major; and the second Tetrachord in the Scale of C Major is the first Tetrachord in the Scale of G Major. Hence, the two Scales related to C are F and G. Work this out on a separate sheet of paper and study it. We will have much use for this principle later on. It lies at the very basis of freedom in creative music.

As an exercise, write out for yourselves the Scales of B♭, E♭, A♭, D♭:

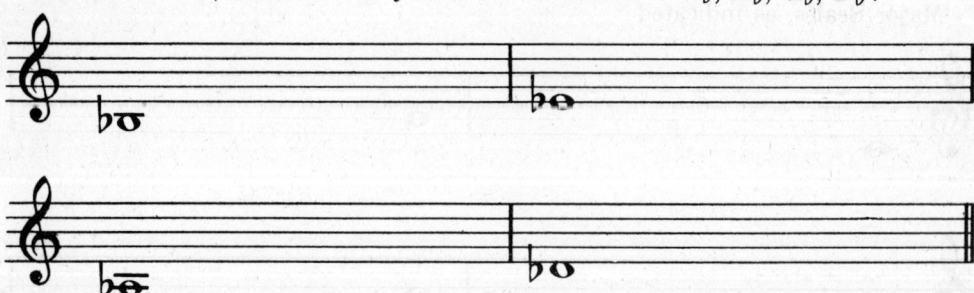

Let us return to the Sharps for a bit and construct a Major Scale on F♯. It is not difficult to accomplish but it will fairly bristle with Sharps. Here are the necessary Degrees:

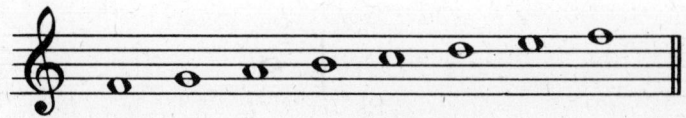

ABOUT THE SCALES

We are beginning with F♯. We know that F to G is a Whole-Step; consequently, if we Sharpen both F and G we will still have a Whole-Step; and this is what we want. In the same manner, if from G to A is a Whole-Step, so it will be from G♯ to A♯. From A♯ is a Half-Step; so our first Tetrachord is correct. We must start our second Tetrachord on C♯, since from B to C♯ is a Whole-Step. We discern readily enough that from C♯ to D♯ is a Whole-Step, but look out for the next one. Our D♯ is correct, but, as it stands we have an E; and there is no black key. Our original theory goes; so, in order to get a Whole-Step, we must call this E♯, and use the white key F, which, for the time being becomes E♯. Thus from E♯ to F♯ is a Half-Step, and our Scale is complete.

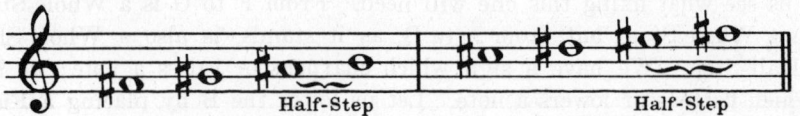

Remember! We cannot change a Letter or cause a skip of a Letter. We can, however, modify a Note by means of Sharps or Flats. These two trick spots in Notation, E to F and B to C, two white piano keys in each case forming a Half-Step, seem to work endless mischief in the minds of students, and sometimes cause slips on the part of experienced writers. Learn about them now and avoid future trouble.

Any Tone that one may seek to indicate is susceptible of being written in several different ways. For instance, we have just learned that E♯ and F are the same in point of Sound (or Pitch). Likewise, in the Scale of F, we were forced to employ a B♭, while the identical sound (Tone) appeared in the F♯ Scale as A♯; a Black Piano Key doing double duty. Such relationships as these are known as **Enharmonic** (a change in Notation without a change of Pitch). The word "Enharmonic" is easy to remember. This device is often at the back of some of the most beautiful effects accomplished in creative music. See what is coming to us, later on!

At this point the student should write out the Major Scales in the order given, placing correctly all the needed Sharps and Flats: C, G, D, A, E, B and C♭, F♯ and G♭, C♯ and D♭, A♭, E♭, B♭, F, C. The Scales B and C♭, F♯ and G♭, C♯ and D♭ are respectively Enharmonic (written, each in two ways, but sounding alike, in each case).

Major Scales, as indicated:

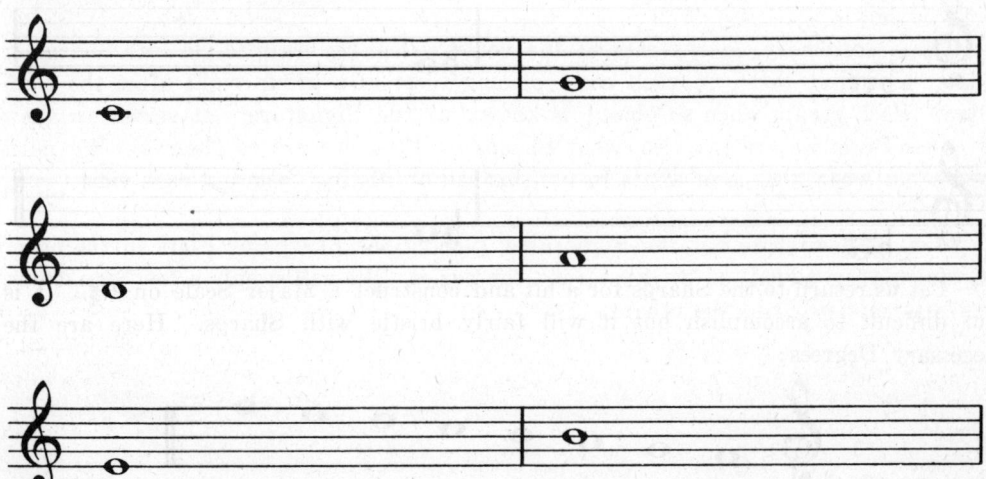

Correct! We started out with the C Major Scale and we wound up with the C Major Scale. This swinging around through the Scales is sometimes called the **Circle of Scales.** It will have been observed, that, as we went on through the Sharps, we added a Sharp, with each new Scale. When we got into the Flats, we took away a Flat, with each new Scale.

It is customary, in the case of the Scales, when we begin to get into Sharps or Flats, to collect them, in each case, placing them in a group right after the Clef-Sign. Each group, when so placed, is known as the **Signature.** It serves to show us what Scale we are in; also, what Sharps or Flats we are to observe. We must remember what Sharps or Flats to use, instead of writing them out each time.

Let us now write out the Signatures, placing the Sharps or Flats in the order in which they added, as we wrote out the Scales. We will supply a few Signatures, the Students will add the others:

ABOUT THE SCALES

There is no royal road to learning. These **must** be learned so that any of them may be written out, on demand. And any or all must be recognized, on sight. Nothing impresses the memory so well as having to write something out. So, write out Scales and Signatures, *ad libitum, ad infinitum!*

QUIZ No. 4

1. What are Related Scales?
2. E♯ and F are the same in point of Sound, although written differently. What is this relationship called?
3. How else (in point of Sound) could we write B♭; E?
4. Between which two pairs of White Piano Keys do we find Half-Steps?
5. What is meant by a Signature?

LESSON FIVE
ABOUT THE INTERVALS

In that typical old-fashioned Harmony Class, about which we told in Lesson Two (maybe not so old-fashioned, at that) we mentioned the assignment of three subjects, at the first lesson. So far, we have just arrived at the end (maybe not the end) of the first of these subjects, and we are about to tackle the second subject: Intervals.

We are now about to place our finger upon the most painful spot in all Harmony study. This will hurt us worse than it does you.

When we move from one Tone to another Tone, differing in Pitch, we create an **Interval**. In this case it is a **Melodic Interval**, because we are in motion as though singing or playing. When we sound together two Tones, differing in Pitch, we create a **Harmonic Interval**. Let the students sing and play some Intervals of their own choosing. Never mind what they are.

For a considerable time, we shall be concerned chiefly with Harmonic Intervals; so, for brevity, we will just use the general term: Interval.

We derive the **Name** of any Interval by counting the number of letters included. For instance: sound C, D together; then, look at the notation:

C, D; two letters are included; hence we call this a **Second**. Never mind what kind of a Second it is: we'll attend to that later.

In a similar manner we may reckon up all of the Intervals to be obtained in a Major Scale, by building up from its first Tone. Take the C Major Scale:

Count all of the letters C, D, E, three letters: a **Third**; C, D, E, F, four letters: a **Fourth**; and so on. This is a simple enough beginning. We do not need the Octave, but we have added it for the sake of completion. We could have added the **Unison** or **Prime**, which occurs when two voices or instruments coincide upon the same Tone, for instance:

You will find many examples in your Hymn Books. Strictly speaking the Unison is not an Interval at all, there being no difference in Pitch.

One cannot conceive of a Harmony student who is unable to sing at sight any one of these elementary Intervals; to name it, when heard; or to write it, on demand. So study them, now. Here is material for splendid eye and ear training. Neglect to master such subjects in the beginning is at the bottom of most failures in Harmony study. By-the-way, no *do, re, mi;* please! This is Music in the abstract, not Sight Singing. At this point, students should write out, in all the Scales, the Intervals complete, as given so far:

ABOUT THE INTERVALS

So far so good!

QUIZ No. 5

1. What is an Interval?
2. What is a Melodic Interval?
3. What is a Harmonic Interval?
4. How do we derive the **Name** of an Interval?
5. What is a Unison?

LESSON SIX

MORE ABOUT THE INTERVALS

It is a peculiar thing about the Intervals that Violinists and Brass Instrument players know more about them from a practical standpoint than do Pianists or Vocalists; and yet, as a rule, those first mentioned are unable to name them; they just know them by feeling or otherwise. Stringed instrument players wander across the strings in all the Positions, measuring the Intervals as they go, usually with just and satisfactory intonation. Professional French Horn players are marvelous in this connection. They play parts written for Horns in all sorts of Scales, all on the Horn in F, transposing at sight the most intricate passages, with scarcely a "sour" Tone. Vocalists, who have been well-trained in their **Solfeggi,** usually get away with it, until matters get too complicated; when, as they cheerfully admit, they read "by Position." The Pianists have everything done for them. They have their beautiful White and Black Keys. But their Sight-Reading would be far more secure if they knew their Intervals better. And the Composers? Oh! Yes, the Composers. We suspect strongly that many of them do their composing right at the Piano Keyboard: the last place in the world for it.

Now, to business! The name of an Interval is one thing, the kind of an Interval is something else. The word **Kind** is applied to an Interval according to the number of Half-Steps one may count up within its limits. In other words—Intervals coincide as to the number of Letters included, but they may differ in the number of Half-Steps to be found therein. Take our initial illustration, the Second. According to our prescription, C-D is a Second; but, so is C-D♭ a Second (also having two letters included). Now, one of these Seconds is smaller than the other. From C to D♭ is only a Half-Step; while from C to D is two Half-Steps (C to D is a Whole-Step, hence, two Half-Steps). To the smaller Second, we apply the term **Minor;** to the larger Second, we apply the term **Major.** All Seconds are designated in this manner, according to the number of Half-Steps. For example:

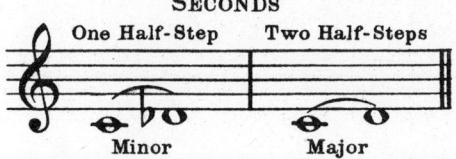

Did someone ask: "May we call from C to C♯ a Second?" No! To make it a Second two Letters are needed. This is a case of **Musical Spelling.** There is only one correct way for spelling each respective Group of Tones used in Music. We are now at the beginning of it.

Let us return to the Series of Intervals which we built up, starting, in each case from the first Degree of the C Major Scale. The Intervals thus formed from the successive Tones of the Major Scale are all either Major Intervals or Perfect Intervals. Occasion will offer a little later for making clear the use of the term **Perfect.** It is applied only to Fourths and Fifths. The point is now to learn the number of Half-Steps included in each of these model Intervals. Here is the Table:

NAME AND KIND OF INTERVAL:

Please count up these Half-Steps, in each Interval and memorize them. Abundant use will be had for them later on. The best grounded Harmony student is the one who knows his Intervals best.

The Intervals thus formed, as in the above Table, are known as the **Normal Intervals** of the Major Scale. They afford splendid practice in Ear- and Eye-Training. In such practice, always call the Intervals by the full-names, such as: Major Second, Perfect Fourth, and so on.

For our present purposes, these are all the Intervals we will need. We will come back, a little later, more strongly than ever. At this point the student should write complete Tables, as above, of the Normal Intervals in each Major Scale.

MORE ABOUT THE INTERVALS

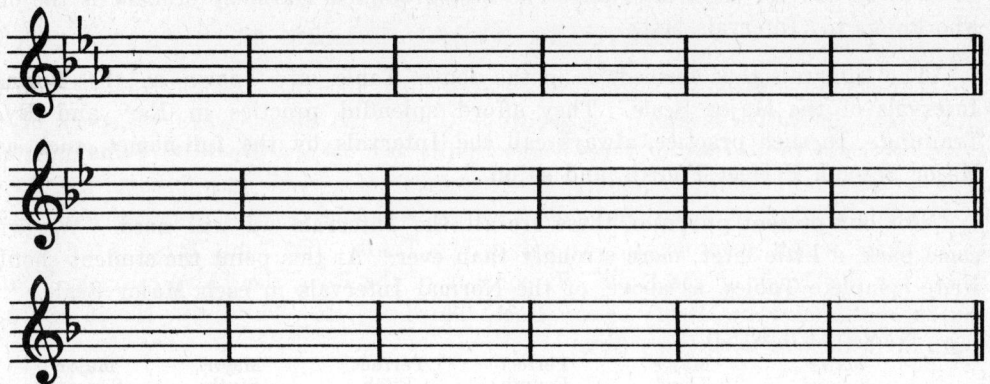

QUIZ No. 6

1. What is meant by the **Kind** of an Interval?
2. Building a series of Intervals over the First Degree of a Major Scale will give us what **Kinds** of Intervals?
3. What is the general name for these (above mentioned) Intervals?
4. As applied to Intervals, what is meant by the terms Major, Minor?
5. How many Half-Steps in a Minor Second?
6. How many Half-Steps in a Major Second?

LESSON SEVEN
SOMETHING ABOUT TRIADS

Scarcely any Music Student escapes very long, hearing about Triads (a funny little Greek derivative meaning: a group of three). In music, when we speak of a **Triad**, we refer to a group of three Tones, built up over a Root or **Fundamental Tone**, in a certain definite manner. Each member of a Scale may become the Root or Fundamental of a Triad, but just now we will stick to the first Degree of the Major Scale, which, from now on, we will call its **Tonic**. The **Tonic Triad** is the Triad built over the Tonic of the Scale. It consists of the Root, the Third over the Root, and the Fifth over the Root; briefly Root, Third, Fifth. The Tonic Triad in the C Major Scale will be written thus:

In Group Music Instruction, Class Piano Teaching and other Elementary Work, more or less is said about Triads. There are many methods of approach and presentation, but, in the end, all reach the same point. Until we reach Harmony itself, we need not disagree much as to names and terms. When so many earnest teachers are working for definite results, certain discrepancies are due to ensue. No work, well done, is ever lost; nothing once learned is ever lost.

To get back to that Triad that we have formed: it is often deserted, just at this point; but let us look at it again:

Here's where some of the real fun of Harmony begins. An innocent little Triad: Root, Third, Fifth. All right! What kind of a Third is it from C to E? A Major Third. Good! And what kind of Fifth is it from C to G? A Perfect Fifth. Good again! Because it has a Perfect Fifth it is considered to be a **Perfect Triad**. And, more important yet, because it has a Major Third, we call it a **Major Triad**. It is known generally as the C Major Triad.

Just for instance: supposing we had written this Triad with an E♭, thus:

Then what? Well, the Third from C to E♭ must be a **Minor Third,** since it is one Half-Step less than a Major Third. Count the Half-Steps. Four of them in a Major Third; three, in a Minor Third. Then here we have a Minor Triad. But we are getting ahead of our story!

Here is an exercise. Write the Tonic Triad in each Scale here, just as we have started it: We give the Signature, you locate the Tonic and write the Triad:

SOMETHING ABOUT TRIADS

Eye- and Ear-Training, as usual.

QUIZ No. 7

1. What is a Triad?
2. Describe the making of a Triad.
3. Build Triads over F; G.
4. What distinguishes a Perfect Triad?
5. What is the difference between a Major Triad and a Minor Triad?
6. What is meant by the Tonic Triad?

LESSON EIGHT

TRIADS AND INTERVALS

We have often thought that Triads and Intervals might, to an extent, be considered together. We might be able to promote an easier understanding of certain matters. Let's try it!

First of all, we will construct a Triad on each Degree of the C Major Scale:

Next, to examine these Triads, and see what can be found: No. 1, we know all about. No. 2 looks all right but, what of the Third from D to F? Three Half-Steps only, hence it is a Minor Third, the Fifth (D to A) is perfect (seven Half-Steps); so this is a Minor Triad. The Intervals are coming in already. Take No. 3: E to G is a Minor Third (three Half-Steps), E to B is a Perfect Fifth (seven Half-Steps); so here we find another Minor Triad. Take No. 4: F to A is a Major Third (four Half-Steps), F to C is a Perfect Fifth (seven Half-Steps); so here again we have a Major Triad. Take No. 5: G to B is a Major Third (four Half-Steps), G to D is a Perfect Fifth (seven Half-Steps); so here we have another Major Triad. Next, No. 6: from A to C is a Minor Third (three Half-Steps), A to E is a Perfect Fifth (seven Half-Steps); hence, at this point we find another Minor Triad. Look out for this next one! No. 7 embraces those two bad spots in Notation and on the Keyboard where we find those Half-Steps E to F, B to C, about which we have given previous warning. Now, see what happens! B to D is a Minor Third (three Half-Steps). So far, so good. But examine the Fifth from B to F. How many Half-Steps here? **Six.** Hence, this is not a Perfect Fifth, and if it is not a Perfect Fifth, it must be an **Imperfect** Fifth. Hence this is an **Imperfect Triad**; and we will leave it at that, for the present; having no particular use for it just now.

We deduce from the foregoing the fact that, in a Major Scale, the Triads on the First, Fourth and Fifth Degrees are Major Triads; those on the Second, Third and Sixth Degrees are Minor Triads. This is one of the most important things to remember so far. Learn it by rote; and **know** it, both by the Eye and the Ear. Just **think** about that Imperfect Triad: one of the stumbling blocks in Musical Theory, as we shall discover later.

Now, as an exercise, the student should fill up the following Table of Triads, in various Scales:

TRIADS AND INTERVALS

STUDENT'S HARMONY BOOK

Much Eye- and Ear-Training may be had from this Table. Make use of it.

Now, not to forget our Intervals; we would like some practice with Major and Minor Thirds. We will give the Major Thirds first, and beside them, the student will write the Minor Thirds. Then, we will give the Minor Thirds, and beside these the student will write the Major Thirds.

This will prove highly interesting, requiring quick and accurate thinking. Remember, you **must not change** a Letter. You may use a ♯ or a ♭ where needed; and you may use the **Natural** or **Cancel** (♮) to "wipe out" a ♯ or ♭ where necessary. When in doubt, count the Half-Steps. Count them, anyway! For example: suppose we have the Major Third: C to E; we will change it to Minor by lowering the E to E♭. But, supposing we had the Major Third: D to F♯; we only need to do away with the ♯ before F, and make it F♮ to produce our Minor Third. Count the Half-Steps, and think it over in each case. Never alter the lower note. Here are a few, for illustration:

Use no Signatures this time. Let's have the actual Notation.

Now, go ahead!:

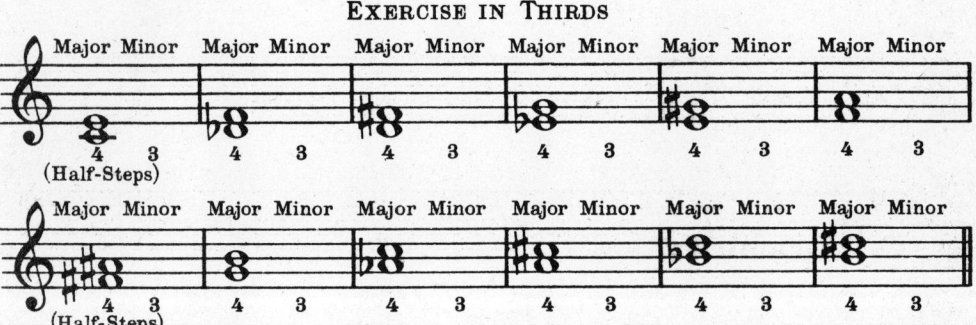

Now, the Minor Thirds will be given; the Student will change them to Major:

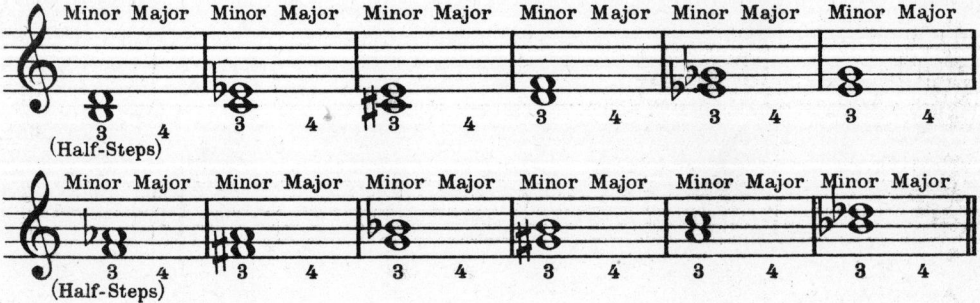

If the student writes these exercises correctly, he will know more about Intervals, especially Thirds, than he ever did before, and much will have been added to the sure Harmonic foundation that we are endeavoring to establish.

QUIZ No. 8

1. In any Major Scale, what Triads are Major; what Triads are Minor?
2. What of the Triad on the Seventh Degree?
3. What is the Major Third over D; over E♭; over F♯?
4. What is the Minor Third over C; B; B♭?
5. How many Half-Steps in a Minor Third; in a Major Third?

LESSON NINE
MORE ABOUT TRIADS

In Elementary Classes, Group Instruction work and in Piano Classes, much seems to be made of the Triads. In actual Harmony teaching, however, we are not so much concerned with them, except to establish their structures and properties in the minds of students, in preparation for more important matters. When the Triad, with its Root doubled (used twice) becomes a **Four-Part Common Chord**, we are then vitally interested. But, once again, we are running a little ahead of our story.

In class work, as aforesaid, there has arisen a little mix-up in terminology. Many teachers prefer to speak of the Three Positions of a Triad. In the light of our treatment of the Four-Part Chord (with which we are now about to have so much to do), two of these Positions **might** be considered as Inversions (something that we are not yet supposed to have heard of). Perhaps all will be satisfied if we state merely that any Triad may be written in **Three Ways.** At any rate, we have little use for them in our Harmony work, although they do serve as valuable bases for technical work on the Piano and other instruments; likewise later on, in forms of accompaniment. Are all agreed? We hope so!

Here is the C Major Triad, written in Three Ways:

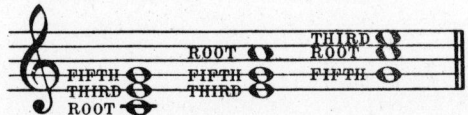

This is all there is to it. Go ahead, and write Triads for yourselves in the Scales here prescribed. We will give the First Way, the students write in the other Two Ways. This is good practice:

MORE ABOUT TRIADS

In Ear-Training, it will prove most helpful to endeavor to recognize, when heard, the particular way in which any given Triad is placed. Which member is at the bottom, which member is at the top, which member is in the middle? It will prove easier, if the members of each given Triad, be sounded slowly, one after the other.

We are, by no means, through with the Intervals. Keep reviewing, most carefully, those already known.

QUIZ No. 9

1. In how many ways may a Triad be written?
2. How is this done?
3. How do we obtain a Four-Part Common Chord?
4. Name the Roots of the following Triads:

LESSON TEN

ABOUT COMMON CHORDS

At last! Now we are getting down to real business. It is customary, as a basis for teaching, and, later on, for composition, or creative music, to regard Harmony as planned and written for four Voices or four Instruments; hence, we speak usually of Four-Part Harmony. When, in the preceding Lesson, we spoke of expanding the Triad into a Four-Part Common Chord, this is what we had in mind. Let us use the word **Chord** or **Common Chord** from now on. Although any member may be doubled in order to complete a Four-Part Common Chord, the Root is the best to use, thus:

It is customary to write Four-Part Harmony on two staves. In such case the original Position of the Chord here given may be distributed in two ways. With the Root in the Bass, in each instance, we may write the Chord with the remaining three Parts in the G clef as close together as possible (within the space of an octave); or we may write two voices on each clef with the notes of the chord more evenly divided. The first of these methods is known as **Close Harmony**; the second, as **Open Harmony**. Please forget about the latter for some time to come. Here is how they look:

In Close Harmony, it is possible to write the Common Chord in three Positions, retaining its Root in the Bass. Thus:

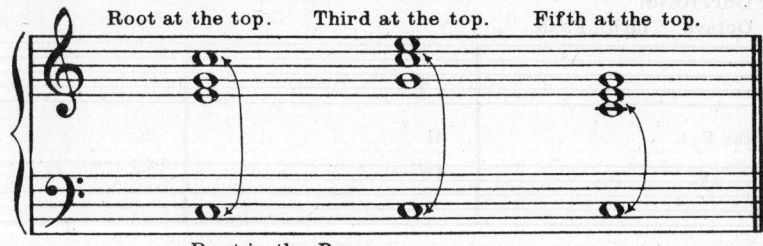

Root in the Bass

When so written, these three Positions are known, respectively, as the **Root** (or **Octave**) Position; the **Third Position;** and the **Fifth Position**: depending upon which member of the Chord is at the top (the Root remaining always in the Bass).

Play these three Positions over many times; compare them; **learn to distinguish** them when heard; consider the effect of each. We are now at the beginning of Creative Music; and we seek beauty. We have always thought that a class in Harmony might be conducted almost as a class in Musical Appreciation also. There should be no dull grind at any time. Music is a joyous Art. A Chord in the **Root Position** seems **full of Repose;** in the **Third Position**, the Chord is rather **Graceful,** slightly **Sad;** the Fifth Position is **Bright,** with a suggestion of **Something to Come.**

ABOUT COMMON CHORDS

We acknowledge freely that Harmony was once upon a time a deadly dull subject, following a cut and dried routine. We were even asked to do without the Piano. Not so, now! Use the Piano all you like for trying things; but not for constructing. Use your voices; use other instruments.

Now, for an Exercise: Write out in full each of the Common Chords on the six Degrees of the Major Scale, each Chord in the Three Positions; omit the Chord on the seventh Degree, with its Imperfect Fifth. Here goes!

Now, do exactly the same things in the Scale of F:

STUDENT'S HARMONY BOOK

And in the Scale of G:
POSITIONS:
Octave Third Fifth

Roots: G | A | B

C | D | E

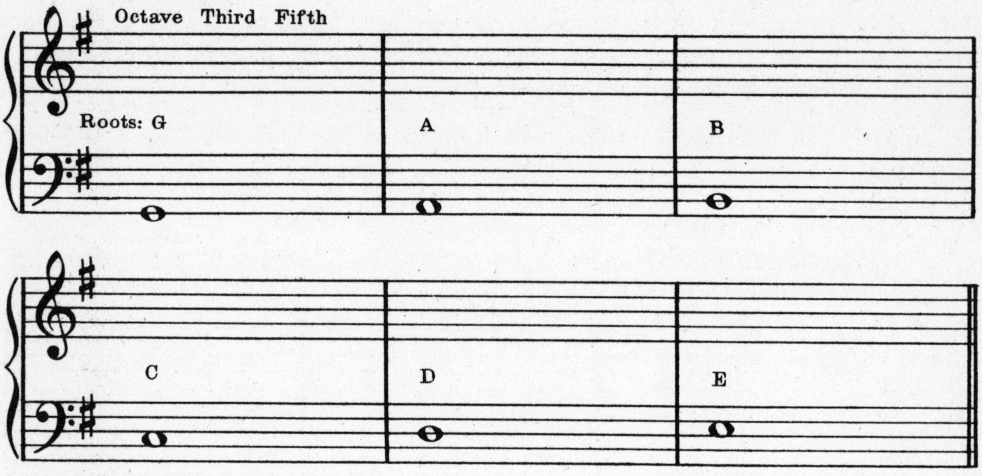

And in the Scale of B♭:
POSITIONS:
Octave Third Fifth

Roots: B♭ | C | D

E♭ | F | G

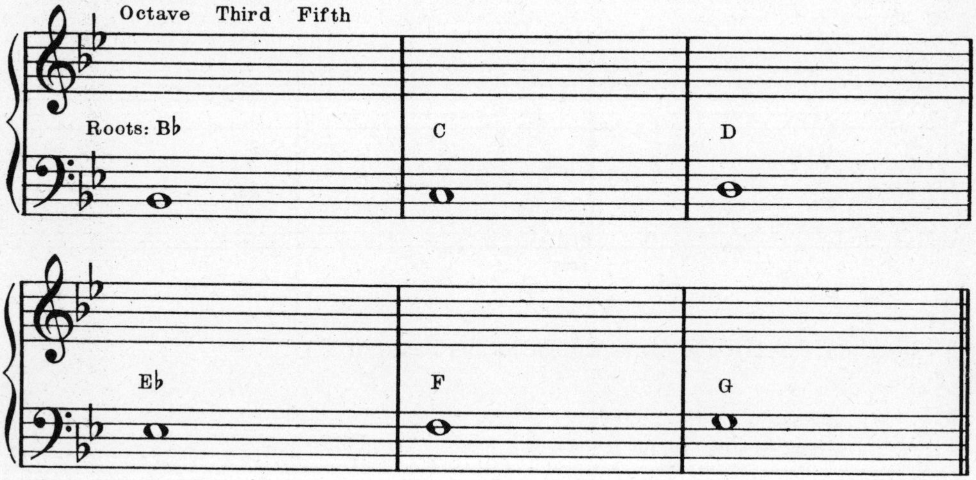

And in the Scale of D:
POSITIONS:
Octave Third Fifth

Roots: D | E | F♯

G | A | B

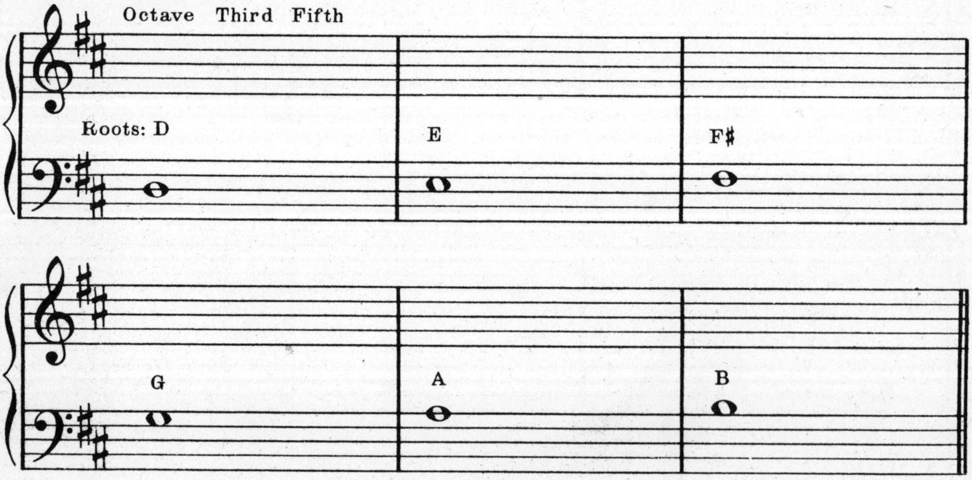

ABOUT COMMON CHORDS

At last, we are are getting somewhere.

QUIZ No. 10

1. What is meant by Four-Part Harmony?
2. What Member of the Common Chord is usually Doubled?
3. Describe Close Harmony; Open Harmony.
4. In Close Harmony, in how many Positions may a Common Chord be written?
5. Name these Positions.
6. How do we get them?
7. Describe the effect of each Position, from the standpoint of Expression.

LESSON ELEVEN
MAKING SOME USE OF THE COMMON CHORDS

Previous to going into this Lesson, every step that we have taken along the way should be checked up. Nothing should be left that is not thoroughly mastered and understood.

Our object now is to make use of the material already presented; and to learn to write in logical, reasonable **succession** the Six Common Chords derived from the Major Scales. So far, we know these Chords in Three Positions only; in each case, with their respective Roots in the Bass. We have learned that Three of these chords are Major Chords: Three of them are Minor Chords. We have been told that the Chord built upon the First Degree of any Scale is known as its Tonic Chord.

At this stage, we will go a little further with this naming of the Major Common Chords. To return to the Scale, we have named its First Degree the **Tonic**; the Fifth Degree is called the **Dominant;** the Fourth Degree, the Sub-Dominant. "Why?" says someone.

We have always considered that these Scale Names were more applicable to the Chords themselves than to the several Degrees upon which the Chords are built. Let us examine, and answer the question for ourselves. Here are the Degrees of the C Major Scale, with the Degree Names, so far supplied:

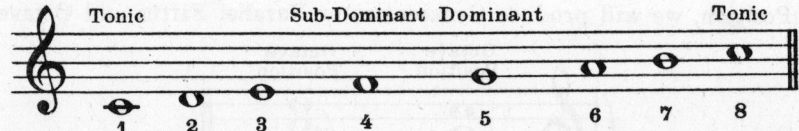

The word Tonic (pertaining to a Tone) is easy enough. The **Tonic** or **Key-Note** names the Scale. The word Dominant means "ruling". We shall soon discover that the **Dominant Chord**, the Chord built upon the Fifth Degree of the Scale is indeed the **Ruling Chord**. The **Sub-Dominant** is easy. The word itself means **under the Dominant**. That is just where it is located. And here are the Three Major Chords, each in its Three Positions, and properly named:

We shall have much to do with these Three Chords, always.

Music is an Art, not a Science; and like "Topsy", in "Uncle Tom's Cabin", "it just growed". We will fight for a **Principle,** but we decline to quarrel over **Definitions**. Principles, Prescriptions, and an occasional Proscription are good for us, however. Music, as we know it, is only about 300 or 400 years old: The youngest of the Arts. Those dear old souls who first experimented with Tones, comparing them, and finally creating Harmonic Intervals, little knew what they were starting. And Monteverde— Well, this is not a Musical History Class! There are many matters pre-

MAKING SOME USE OF THE COMMON CHORDS

scribed for students, to which, later on, exceptions may be taken. But after all, it is only he who is best acquainted with things as they are, who is best equipped to lead us into newer paths.

We will begin with a **Proscription: Do not write two adjacent Common Chords, each having the Root in the Bass, in the same Position.** Why? We shall proceed to demonstrate. When our older theorists were experimenting with the Intervals, they were at first inclined to view Fourths and Fifths with favor; even to the point of employing them consecutively between two voices. Later they ruled that **Consecutive Fifths and Octaves be prohibited**: Consecutive Fifths because they appeared to indicate two different Scales moving at once; Consecutive Octaves, because they created no Harmony. A study of this example may serve to make matters clear:

Try these over on your Piano! Try singing them, also. These examples represent some of the first attempts at writing in parts. Do they remind us, somehow, of "Jazz"? Yes, they do. And "Jazz" reminds us of a number of things, which we will not mention. But what has all of this to do with two or more Chords in the same Position? Just this: that, should we write Common Chords consecutively in the same Position, we will produce Consecutive or **Parallel Fifths** and **Octaves**. For example:

The Fifths and Octaves are occurring between the same two Voices in each Chord. This will be obviated by the change in Position of one of the Chords. In pure Harmony we must pay attention to such matters. The two chords above could have been written more effectively; complying at the same time, with our Proscription:

Make an Ear Test of all these examples. Naturally, using only the Roots of Chords in the Bass, we are somewhat limited in variety for the present. But even the following exercises must be made to sound good. Use your Ears all the time. We have no use for Harmony which remains on paper only.

Oh, yes! The Three Minor Chords. We shall use them somewhat in the following exercises, but place our main reliance on the Major Chords. The Minor Chords give color and variety. We have already named the First, Fourth and Fifth Degrees of the Scale; the remaining Degrees are easy. The Second Degree is called the **Supertonic** (over the Tonic); the Third Degree the **Mediant** (half-way between the Tonic and Dominant); the Sixth Degree, the **Sub-Mediant** (half-way between the Sub-Dominant and Tonic). Never mind the Seventh Degree, as yet; it will cause sufficient trouble, later on. Here are the six Degrees:

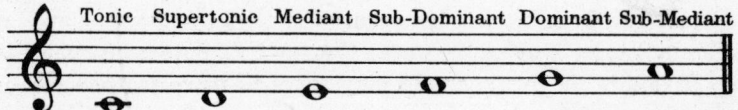

A good Mental Drill may be had by calling off, on demand, the letter names of the various Degrees in other Scales, or **Keys**. We may use the word Key now, having established the word Key-Note. For instance: "Dominant of G?" "D"; "Mediant of F?" "A"; and so on.

Now, let's write! It is a good habit, by-the-way, to retain in the same Parts or Voices, notes common to two successive Chords. They are sometimes called **Binding Tones**. They make for smoothness, thus:

The Binding Tones are tied merely to call attention to them. In trying the exercises, the full Chord is to be played, each time. Proceed, Student! We will start off each Exercise with a Chord or two:

MAKING SOME USE OF THE COMMON CHORDS

All of these should be made to sound. Each one is susceptible of several correct solutions. Write each one over several times, on a separate sheet of paper. It will be noted, that we begin and end, each Exercise, with the Tonic Chord. This is done in order to establish the Scale, the Key, the **Tonality**. Any Position will do for either of these first and last Chords.

QUIZ No. 11

1. What Name is given to the Fifth Degree of the Scale? Why?
2. What is the Fourth Degree called? Why?
3. In writing a series of Common Chords, with Roots in the Bass, what Proscription do we follow?
4. By doing thus, what do we avoid?
5. Why are Consecutives not good?
6. Name the Second Degree of the Scale; the Third Degree; the Sixth Degree.
7. What sort of Chords are the Chords on these Degrees?
8. What are Binding Tones?
9. With what Chord do we begin and end each Exercise?

LESSON TWELVE
SETTING CHORDS TO A MELODY

Many may be wondering why we have not given any Roman Numerals, as yet. We will fight shy of any figured Bass, as long as we may. When the student has learned to **think** Harmony, the Figured Bass (a little of it) may prove a help; at any rate, it can do no harm. We are trying to approach Harmony through inductive reasoning, thinking things out, as we go. Following a pattern is too easy; one learns little.

Now, let us reverse matters, for a bit; and see if we can harmonize a given Melody, employing the knowledge so far attained.

Our material, so far acquired, consists of Six Common Chords, with Roots in the Bass in each case; with Three possible Positions of each Chord.

Since we have been using the Chords in this manner: each, in one of three possible Positions, it stands to reason that any **Melody** (upper part) **Note** may be treated as either the Root, the Third, or the Fifth of some one Chord. Having decided which member of a Chord any given Melody Note is to be, we next locate the Root of the Chord; and, at once, write it in the Bass. The Root, if it is to be a Melody note, settles itself; if the Melody Note is to be the Third of a Chord, we must count down a Third to obtain the Root; if the Melody Note is to be a Fifth, then we count a Fifth to get the Root. That's all there is to it, except to decide which is which, and to decide also, which sounds the best. But do **not** attempt to make that Seventh Degree of the Scale a Root. Begin and end, of course, with the Tonic Chord. Here is a Melody which we will Harmonize, as a sample, and explain:

Let us examine: we know that we are to start on the Tonic Chord, whose Root is C; we have a G in the Melody, which must be the **Fifth** of the Chord, so we will put this down at once, writing in the Bass note first:

The next note, A, may be treated, according to our scheme, as the Third of a Chord, or the Root of a Chord; it must not be a Fifth, as we have just had a Fifth: it may be treated as the Third of the Chord, F-A-C; or the Root of the Chord, A-C-E. Try it, each way. Let us take the first mentioned; then we have:

Now for the third Melody Note, B: we may make it a Fifth only. Why? Our preceding Chord is in the Third Position; this leaves us either the Fifth Position, or the Octave, supposedly, for the next chord, but, we cannot use B (Seventh Degree of the Scale) as a Root; so we must consider B as a Fifth only; and the E becomes the Root; and here we are:

Take the fourth Melody Note: it cannot be a Fifth; but it may be either a Third or a Root, thus:

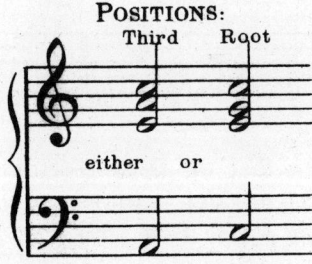

Try them over! we incline to the Third Position. Next, we have the fifth Melody Note, D: we may have an Octave Position, or a Fifth Position:

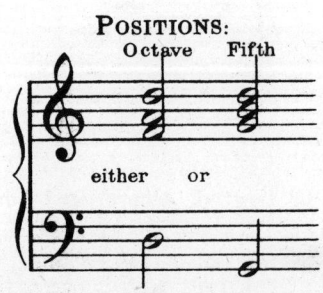

SETTING CHORDS TO A MELODY

Try them. We incline to the Octave Position.

Next, the sixth Melody Note, B: we may have a Third Position, or a Fifth Position:

Try them. We prefer the Third Position.

The final Chord settles itself: we must end on the Tonic: the Octave Position, of course. And here is the complete solution:

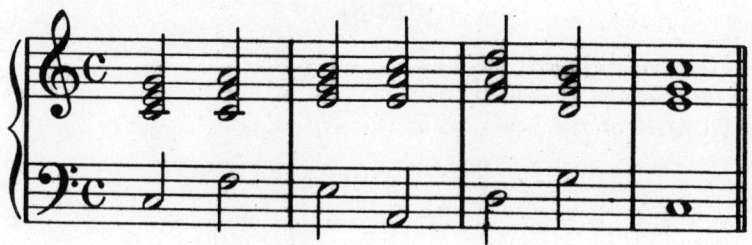

Play, ponder, Analyze. We have used all six of the Common Chords. Now is the Student's chance. See what may be done with these Melodies:

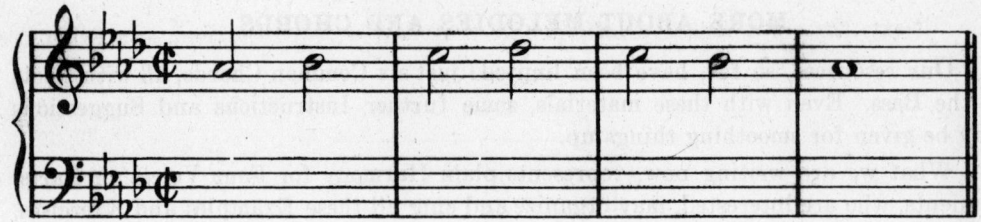

Do not let go of any of these until all sound well.

Have you used any Seventh Degrees as Bass Notes?

QUIZ No. 12
1. What Harmonic material have we, so far?
2. How do we treat Melody notes?
3. What Degree of the Scale cannot be a Bass note, so far?

LESSON THIRTEEN
MORE ABOUT MELODIES AND CHORDS

Our resources, so far, have been limited: just six Common Chords, all with Roots in the Bass. Even with these materials, some further Instructions and Suggestions may be given for smoothing things up.

What we are writing now, represents plain Harmony for Four Voices, or Parts. Students, who are interested, may organize and sing all these Examples and Exercises. We have heard worse. The **Bass,** the lowest part, and the **Melody,** the topmost (or **Soprano**) part represent the **Outer Voices**; the **Alto** and **Tenor** parts, just beneath the **Soprano** part, represent the **Inner Voices.**

As regards writing for Voices, there are certain Customs or Practices that hold good for all time. Both the Outer Parts or Voices moving up or down, in one direction, are said to produce **Parallel Motion; Oblique Motion** obtains when one Part stands still while the other Part moves up or down; **Contrary Motion** means that the Outer Parts are moving in opposite directions. **Contrary Motion** is best; **Oblique Motion** is next best; **Parallel** (or **Similar**) **Motion** is employed when it may seem advisable. Look after these Motions in future writing. Here are some examples:

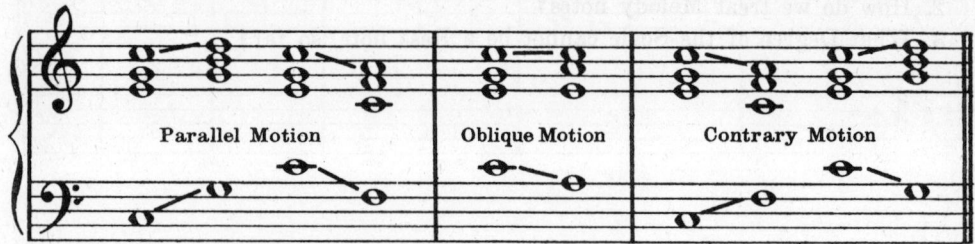

The Bass Part needs watching always. It should have a Melodic character of its own, where possible. It should always be free from awkward Intervals. It should never skip more than a Sixth.

Hidden Octaves or **Fifths** occur, when two Parts (or Voices) move by Parallel Motion to an Octave or to a Fifth, one (or both) of the Parts (or Voices) proceeding by a skip. For example:

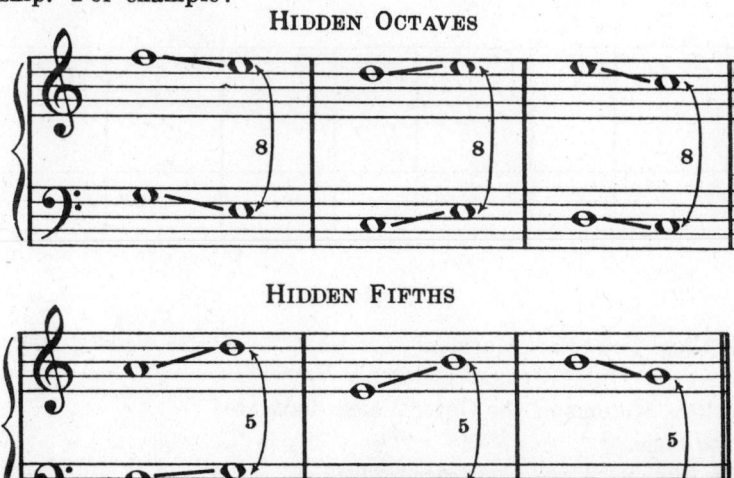

We do not worry much about them, these days. In fact they are used, occasionally, with good effect.

With the addition of these newer directions, and the continued observance of all preceding, these additional Exercises should begin to sound like something. The same Chord may be used twice, in succession, but the Position should change each time. Here is some real work:

QUIZ No. 13

1. In this Close Four-Part Harmony, for what Voices are we writing?
2. What are the Outer Voices? the Inner Voices?
3. What three Motions of the Outer Voices have we?
4. Describe them.
5. What is best; next best; least desirable?
6. How about the Bass Part?
7. What are Hidden Octaves and Fifths?

LESSON FOURTEEN
ABOUT INVERSIONS

There is a certain effect of squareness always in connection with a series of Chords, all having their Roots in the Bass. Harmony, it must be remembered, treats of the motions and the reactions of Tone Groups. We will find, after a while, that it is not necessary to supply a different Chord for every Melody Tone. We are not now trying to write Hymn Tunes either, although we have heard some Hymn Tunes that were not so good Harmonically as some of the Exercises we are doing right now. Some of the books seem to stress the Three Major Chords unduly. This makes for monotony. We need the Minor Chords for contrast. It is not a good thing to impose too many restrictions.

Here is a question one is sometimes asked: "How can we have **Minor** Intervals (and consequently **Minor** Chords) in the **Major Scale?**" We have already explained that. Let's do it again. Only the Intervals built on the **Key-Note** of a Major Scale are all either Major or Perfect. If we build Intervals within the Major Scale, on certain other Degrees, we will find plenty of Minors. The word Major means Greater, only. Intervals are regulated as to **kind,** only by their measurements, by the number of **Half-Steps** included. The **Third** in a Chord tells you whether or not the Chord is Major or Minor. Hammer at the Intervals continually. They are very generally neglected, or misunderstood.

A Common Chord need not always have its Root in the Bass, although it is always safer to use the Root. When we place either the **Third** or the **Fifth** of a Chord in the Bass, we are said to have made an **Inversion** of the Chord. If the **Third** is placed in the **Bass**, we have what is called a **First Inversion**; if the **Fifth**, a **Second Inversion,** thus:

We have recapitulated the Positions, in the first group of our example so as to show the Common Chord in all its aspects. When we place the **Third** in the **Bass**, and thus obtain the **First Inversion,** we may **Double** either the **Root** or the **Fifth** of the Chord. It is unwise to **Double** the **Third**: we will not do so in these exercises. When we place the **Fifth** in the Bass, and thus obtain the **Second Inversion,** we usually **Double** the **Fifth** only. Now try these over, all of them; compare; and begin learning to distinguish them when heard, and to recognize them when seen.

To borrow an expression from Physics: a Chord with its Root in the Bass is like a body in Stable Equilibrium; a Chord with its Third in the Bass, like a body in Neutral Equilibrium (just balanced); a Chord with its Fifth in the Bass, like a body in Unstable Equilibrium (ready to fall, suggesting going somewhere). Think about all this. Again compare!

We will leave the Second Inversion, for the time being; and concentrate upon the **First Inversion**. We have said, that in the First Inversion, either the Root or the Fifth may be Doubled. Here are all of the ways in which this may be done:

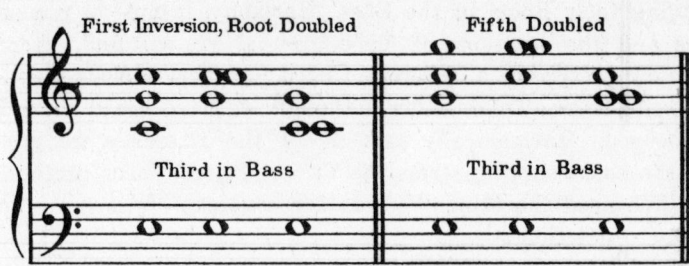

The Unisons (see the 2nd, 3rd, 5th and 6th Chords in our example) indicate two Parts or Voices landing upon the same Degree. This is acceptable, and sometimes very convenient.

Now, as an Exercise, the student will write the First Inversion (six ways, as in our Example) of each of the Chords here given.

ABOUT INVERSIONS

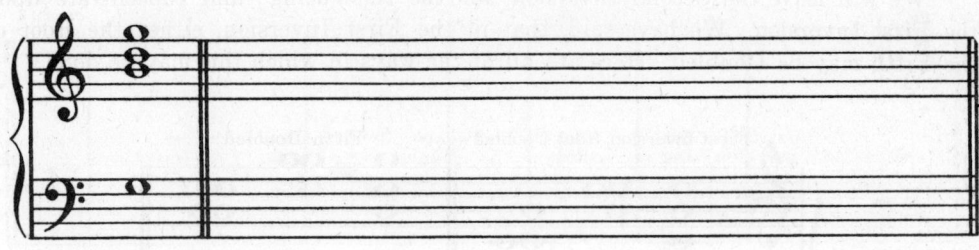

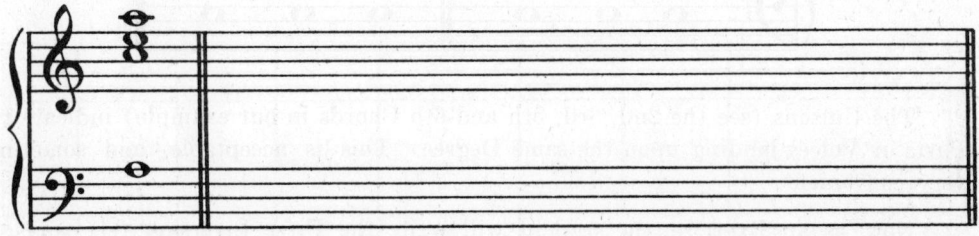

Now, here is an example which the student will please Analyze; every Chord of it. State the Key (or Scale) first. Where not a First Inversion, state the Degree Name and Position of each Chord: wherever a First Inversion simply so state (1st Inv.), indicating the Root. We will mark the first few, to show how it should be done:

A good job! And well done, we hope.

We will go back to Harmonizing Basses, for a little. We will indicate, just at first, where First Inversions are desirable; later on permitting the student to find some for himself. Remember! When planning a First Inversion the Bass note is a Third; next, find the Root and write it in the G clef; then add the Fifth; and Double whichever of these latter seems most advisable. Here are some Exercises which may be made to sound very well indeed:

The Student is now given a chance to locate some First Inversions for himself. It stands to reason that the Seventh Degree of the Scale, when found in the Bass, must be the Third of a Chord, since it cannot be a Root: so here we find a ready-made First Inversion. Look out for it! As a matter of fact, any one of the three Major Chords (Tonic, Dominant or Sub-Dominant) are easy to handle in the First Inversion. Of course, one must watch the Positions of Chords, when Roots are in the Bass, just as before; but a First Inversion may follow any Position, provided the Prescription regarding Similar, Oblique and Contrary Motion be observed; also, it is well to watch out for Binding Tones, just as usual. Now, go ahead:

ABOUT INVERSIONS

All of these **must** sound well. They will go very smoothly, if sufficient pains are taken. We are beginning to make music now.

QUIZ No. 14

1. What do you mean by an Inversion of a Chord?
2. How many are there? Describe each.
3. In the First Inversion, what members of a Chord may be "doubled"?
4. What will you do with the Seventh Degree of the Scale, when found in the Bass?
5. In the Second Inversion, what Member is best to double?
6. Compare the physical conditions of a Chord in a Position, in a First Inversion, in a Second Inversion.

LESSON FIFTEEN
MORE ABOUT THE FIRST INVERSION

We have no use in Harmony for anything that does not Sound; and Sound well, at that. Nor have we any use for the type of music to which may be applied Mark Twain's dictum: "They tell me some music is better than it sounds."

Enough! let's get to work and improve upon our own efforts. It is possible to use First Inversions in succession by Doubling in the Octave in the upper voices in one Chord, and in the Unison in the succeeding Chord, thus:

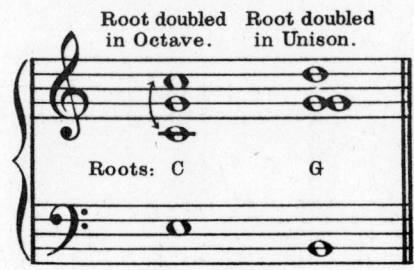

It is possible also to Double the Root in one First Inversion, and the Fifth in the next:

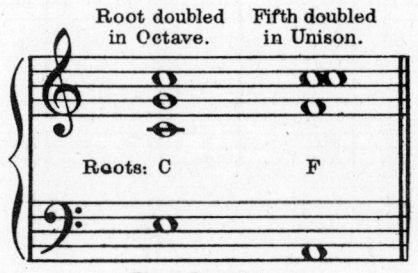

In both of these cases we have acted so as to avoid Consecutive Fifths and Octaves, as explained previously. We must keep our Four-Part writing pure and beyond criticism. In addition to the sensuous pleasure to be derived from Music, there is also an intellectual delight to be derived from beauty of construction.

Here is an Example, with instances of the employment of our added resources. All previous directions are in full force:

MORE ABOUT THE FIRST INVERSION

Now, the student will analyze this Example, using the space below. Each Chord is lettered. Please give, on the corresponding line, the Root of each Chord, together with its Position or Inversion:

(a)

(b)

(c)

(d)

(e)

(f)

(g)

(h)

(i)

(j)

(k)

(l)

(m)

(n)

(o)

This is fine practice. Play and sing, of course.

And here is another exercise for the student. Do as you like with it, but make it acceptable:

This is a sturdy sort of a Bass; it is possible to contrive a very good melody in the outer part above it; see if you can do it. Do not quit until you have won!

QUIZ No. 15
1. How may we manage to use two First Inversions of Chords in succession?
2. What do we avoid by so doing?
3. What two sources of pleasure are to be found in Music?
4. Describe the above.

LESSON SIXTEEN
ABOUT THE SECOND INVERSION

We are by no means through with the First Inversion. In fact, we shall never be through with the Common Chords in their Positions and Inversions. These constitute the "bread and butter" of music.

The Second Inversion is a sort of a bugbear. Many composers, otherwise capable and well trained, seem not to know what to do with it. We believe this to be because sufficient attention is not given it in the very beginning. It is, after all, not so much what one does with a Second Inversion as what one refrains from doing. The Second Inversion is not to be used promiscuously. Of the Second Inversions of the Common Chords, that of the Tonic is by far the most useful. We will stick to this one for the present. Take the three ways in which it is possible to write the Second Inversion of the Tonic in the key of C Major:

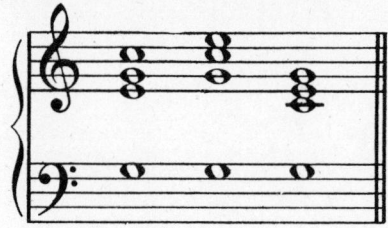

At first sight, as suggested by some students, they look like Positions, but, not having the Root in the Bass, we cannot speak of them in this manner. Inversions cannot have Positions. Play these three forms of the Second Inversion of the Tonic. They all seem to lean, or to look forward; they cannot stand alone. That's just it; another Chord is needed. Try the Dominant Chord in a suitable Position, in each case, and then we have:

All very good! But the Dominant Chord, having propped up the Second Inversion of the Tonic, seems, in turn, to wish to go somewhere, itself. Very well! Let it go to the Tonic (in a suitable Position). The Dominant always tends towards the Tonic; as we shall find out more specifically, later on. Thus, we have:

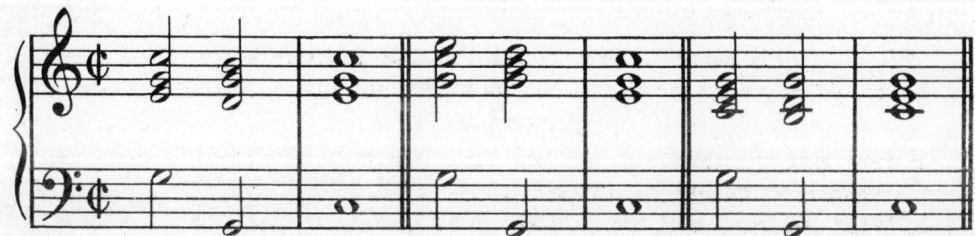

ABOUT THE SECOND INVERSION

Nothing easier, if one could only think of it at the right time; and also remember, never to leave that Second Inversion "standing out in the cold". We shall have more to say about this particular Succession of Chords, later on. Meanwhile, we might add still another Chord. It so happens that either the Supertonic Chord (remember: on the Second Degree of the Scale), or the Sub-Dominant Chord, will be found very effective, to precede the Second Inversion of the Tonic. If so used, either of these Chords may be in a suitable Position, or in some form of a First Inversion. For instance:

There we are! Four Chords in a row: all "cut and dried". But it's "up to the student" to Analyze this Example for himself.

Now, for an Exercise or two, in which the Student will employ all resources, so far attained, including the Second Inversion of the Tonic Chord:

STUDENT'S HARMONY BOOK

QUIZ No. 16

1. What Common Chord is best to use in the Second Inversion?
2. What Chord is best with which to follow a Second Inversion of the Tonic Chord?
3. What Chords are best to precede a Second Inversion of the Tonic?
4. What series of four Chords might then ensue?

LESSON SEVENTEEN
ABOUT NUMERALS AND FIGURES AND THEIR APPLICATION

We could teach Harmony without a single Numeral, Figure, or other indication; and, very likely, do it better; we bow to convention, however. We insist, nevertheless, that every step be worked out, first of all, by inductive reasoning, before anything in the nature of Figures be applied. We will learn the thing itself, first.

Figured Bass (sometimes called **Thorough Bass**) is, after all, a system of Shorthand, very good in its place, and very useful, if not abused. By the use of the Figured Bass, in which certain Numerals and Figures are employed, singly or in combination, it is possible to indicate the Chords, their Positions and their Inversions. We will introduce the Figured Bass, with due reserve, wherever it may prove helpful; but never, before we have developed our subject thoroughly.

Through various matters, taken up in elementary class work, many students today have a knowledge of the use of the **Roman Numerals**. These are used to indicate the Degrees of the Scale; and hence the Roots of Chords. Large-sized Numerals are used to indicate the Roots of Major Chords; smaller-sized Numerals, for the Roots of Minor Chords. The Six Common Chords in C Major would be indicated as follows:

Do not worry about the Seventh Degree, just yet.

The student has probably guessed the Figures for the Three Positions of the Common Chord. They are: 8 (Octave Position); 3 (Third Position); 5 (Fifth Position).

The First and Second Inversions of the Common Chords are indicated very simply: 6 for the First Inversion; $\frac{6}{4}$ for the Second Inversion. We knew it! Now it comes! "Why the 6; why the $\frac{6}{4}$?" The books all seem to fight shy of the reasoning, but here it is: suppose you have this:

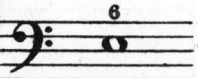

The 6 being the sign of a First Inversion, we know that the E cannot be the Root, but must be a Third. Still, that does not explain the 6; but, if we will count up the Interval of a **Sixth** from E, we will find C, which is to be considered the Root of the Chord. This may take a little thought, but it is the rational manner of studying it out. Of course, if the Numeral were there, we would know the Root, in any event:

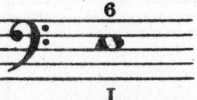

But in cases like this we do not bother to write the **Numeral**.

The Figures for the Second Inversion ($\frac{6}{4}$) are explained similarly:

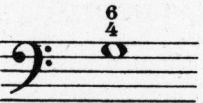

Count up a **Fourth** from G and we will have C, the Root of this Second Inversion; a Sixth from G will give E, the Third of this same Chord.

Figuring is but a system of "measuring". It has naught to do with the derivation of any Chord. Figures merely indicate certain Intervals, counted up from a Bass Note, not necessarily a Root.

Without going further, and without any additional explanation, the student should be able to work out for himself, the following Figured Basses.

In addition to the Inversions, a few Positions are indicated:

ABOUT NUMERALS AND FIGURES AND THEIR APPLICATION

And now, for a Melody or two! In addition to the Figures, we will give the Roman Numerals. All these latter indicate Roots of Chords: the Roots are to be Bass notes, except where Inversions are indicated. A little more thought may be needed here:

STUDENT'S HARMONY BOOK

We are progressing!

QUIZ No. 17

1. What do we mean by Figured Bass?
2. Describe the use of the Roman Numerals.
3. What Figures do we use for the Three Positions of a Chord?
4. Explain the Figuring for the First, and for the Second Inversion.

LESSON EIGHTEEN
MORE ABOUT THE SECOND INVERSION

The proper uses of the Second Inversion need to be stressed. So far we have dealt only with the Tonic $\frac{6}{4}$, as it is so often called. The **Sub-Dominant** and the **Dominant** Chords (IV and V) may appear occasionally in the Second Inversion, if introduced carefully. The Second Inversion needs to be introduced through another Chord, and ushered out through still another Chord before the effect is entirely satisfactory. Just here is where so many Composers lose out.

Take the Sub-Dominant Chord in the Second Inversion. It sounds best only when preceded by the Tonic Chord and followed by the Tonic Chord; the Tonic Chord, in either case, being in one of the Positions. Not much else may be done with the Sub-Dominant $\frac{6}{4}$. This is the way to do it:

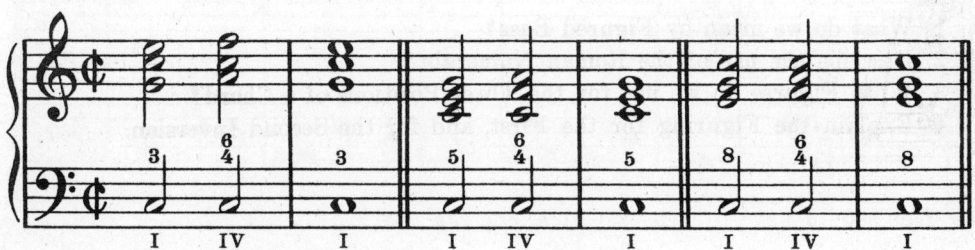

Just as easy as can be! The thing is, to remember it.

The Second Inversion of the Dominant is very interesting. There is only one way in which to work it to advantage: precede it with the First Inversion of the Tonic and follow it with a suitable Position of the Tonic or contrariwise. This is the manner in which it is done:

Here are some Figured Basses, in which are given opportunities for the use of First and Second Inversions (6 and $\frac{6}{4}$ Chords). All the resources so far attained may be brought into play:

This should have proven easy; but one can never tell.

Here is another Bass (Unfigured). Let us see what the student can do, on his own hook:

MORE ABOUT THE SECOND INVERSION

And here's a Melody, all Unfigured:

And that's that!

QUIZ No. 18

1. Describe the use of the Second Inversion of the Sub-Dominant Chord.
2. Describe the use of the Second Inversion of the Dominant Chord.

LESSON NINETEEN
ABOUT THE MINOR SCALE
More Intervals

We have never yet met a student who knew the Intervals too well. In this book we have divided them up a bit, with the hope that by giving them in smaller doses, they might arrive at better comprehension in the end. We are taking them up as needed. As will speedily appear, the introduction of the Minor Scale will bring with it some additional Intervals, account of which must be taken.

The **Minor Scale** is an older form of Scale which we have grown accustomed to treat as related to the Major Scale. In other words, each Major Scale is considered as having a **Relative Minor Scale,** each possessing the same Signature. This works out very well in practice, once it is understood.

The **Tonic** or **Key-Note** of each **Minor Scale** is located upon the Sixth Degree of its Relative Major Scale. For instance, the Sixth Degree of C Major is A; hence A Minor is the Relative Minor of C Major. In order to write out the original Minor Scale, we simply rearrange the Tones of the Major Scale, beginning on the Sixth Degree. Here we are:

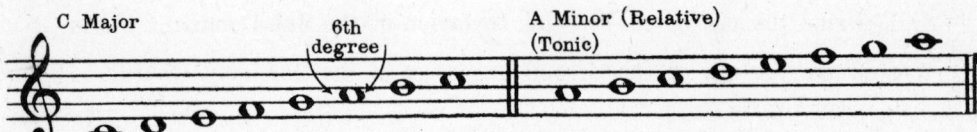

The form of Minor Scale given above is the **Ancient** or **Natural** form of this Scale. The needs of our Harmonic system, however, require that we alter this Scale slightly by **Raising** its Seventh Degree, **one Half-Step.** When we do this, the Scale becomes known as the **Harmonic Minor Scale**: it is the form with which we have most to do in Harmony. So as not to confuse matters, we will deal with no other form at present. Here it is:

We will now name the **Seventh Degree** of any Scale; this applies either in the Major or in the Minor Scale; it is called the **Leading Note.** We have a natural Leading Note in the Major Scale (one Half-Step below the Tonic), but in the Minor Scale it is needful to create one. This alteration of a Note, by **Raising** it (or **Lowering** it) one **Half-Step** is known as a **Chromatic** alteration. More about this later.

ABOUT THE MINOR SCALE

Here are the C Major Scale, and its Relative, the A Minor Scale, with their Leading Notes indicated:

The Leading Note will be found to be of much importance from now on.

Take notice, that in supplying a Leading Note for the Minor Scale, we have created an Interval upon which we have not touched previously: the Interval created by the Sixth and Seventh Degrees of the Harmonic Minor Scale: F to G♯. What is it? From F to G is a Major Second (two Half-Steps); then, from F to G♭ would be a Minor Second (one Half-Step). We shall have to invent a name for F to G♯ (three Half-Steps). When we **raise Chromatically** an Interval already either Major or Perfect, we will call it an **Augmented Interval**. The Interval now in question (F to G♯) is an **Augmented Second**. Our collection of Intervals is growing. Here are the Seconds:

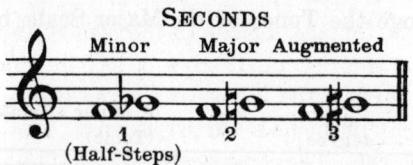

The term **Minor**, as applied alike to Intervals, Scales or Chords, means merely, Lesser. Learn to know the Sound of all these Minor Intervals, Scales and Chords.

Perforce, we must return to Triads; but this time, the **Triads** to be found in the **Harmonic Minor Scale.** Let's have a look at them:

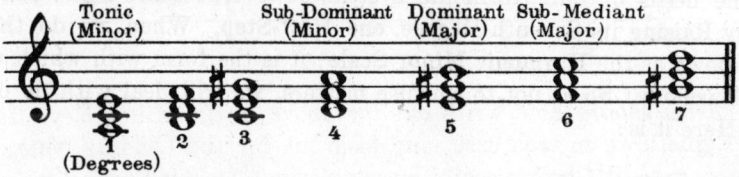

In this lot we can find material for only four **Perfect Common Chords.** Two of them are **Minor**; the **Tonic** and the **Sub-Dominant.** Two of them are **Major**: the **Dominant** and the **Sub-Mediant.**

What of the others? The **Supertonic** contains an **Imperfect Fifth**; the **Mediant** contains an **Augmented Fifth** (a Fifth, greater than a Perfect Fifth; as already mentioned in this Lesson); the **Leading Note Chord** has another Imperfect Fifth. And there we are.

We can now, once more, discuss some Intervals; and especially the term Perfect as applied to Intervals. We once knew a Theorist who declaimed solemnly: "Fourths and Fifths are called Perfect because they do not admit of Mutation." Puzzle out this one! Meanwhile, we are told also, that Fourths and Fifths are called Perfect because, if inverted they remain Perfect. Very lucid indeed! The point is, that the ancient Theorists deemed Fourths and Fifths the only Perfect Intervals; since, if altered Chromatically they became Imperfect. Seconds, Thirds, Sixths and Sevenths are just as good, whether Major or Minor. Music makes its own definitions as it goes along.

The Perfect Fourth has five Half-Steps; the Perfect Fifth has seven Half-Steps. We can **Augment** each; and we can **Diminish** each. Thus:

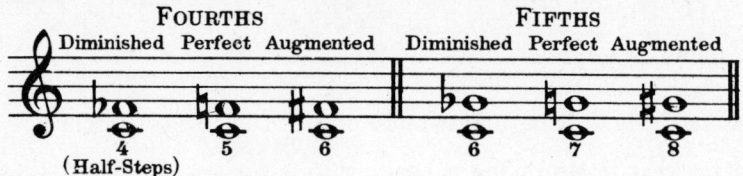

There they are. These should cause no further misunderstandings. They are to be considered separate and apart from the other Intervals. Bear in mind **always**, that the **Fifth** over the **Leading Note** (Seventh Degree of any Scale) is a Diminished Fifth (six Half-Steps: count them). It will be noted that the Augmented Fourth and the Diminished Fifth have each the same number of Half-Steps. These must always be written correctly and never substituted, one for the other. Correct "spelling" must be observed, always. Our Table of Intervals is still growing. Learned as needed, in this practical manner, they should certainly stick.

Here are the Numerals for the Triads in the Minor Key. We give them here for A Minor. The Numeral for the Second Degree is II°, indicating a Diminished Triad (containing a Diminished Fifth); the Numeral for the Diminished Triad or the Leading Note (also containing Diminished Fifth) is VII°. The smaller cipher (°) indicates the Diminished Interval. The Numeral for the Mediant Triad is III′, indicating an Augmented Triad (containing an Augmented Fifth). The accent (′) indicates the Augmented Interval. Here we are, complete:

The Student, should now write out the above in the Minor Keys, as indicated. Supply the Signatures, in each case; and look out for the Leading Note; if it is already a Sharp, raise it Chromatically by supplying a **Double-Sharp** (×); if it should happen to be a ♭, raise it Chromatically by using a **Cancel** or **Natural** (♮). The Letter must never be changed. For practice, write in the Numerals each time. Here goes!

ABOUT THE MINOR SCALE

Check up on these! Are the Leading Notes correct? How about ♯, 𝄪, ♮? The Leading Note appears three times in each series of Triads.

QUIZ No. 19

1. How do we obtain the Minor Scale?
2. What is meant by the term Relative Minor?
3. What is the oldest form of the Minor Scale?
4. How do we construct the Harmonic Minor Scale?
5. What is the Seventh Degree of any Scale called?
6. By giving the Minor Scale a Leading Note, what Interval do we create?
7. Describe the three Kinds of Seconds that we now have.
8. How many Half-Steps in each of these Seconds?
9. How many Perfect Common Chords in the Minor Scale?
10. Which are Minor? Which are Major?
11. What of the remaining Chords?
12. What about Fourths and Fifths, and how are they modified?
13. Give the Numerals for the Triads in the Minor Scale.

LESSON TWENTY
USING MINOR HARMONIES

Now for a little practice in the Minor Key. We will stick to the possible Perfect Common Chords, for the present. They are, in A Minor:

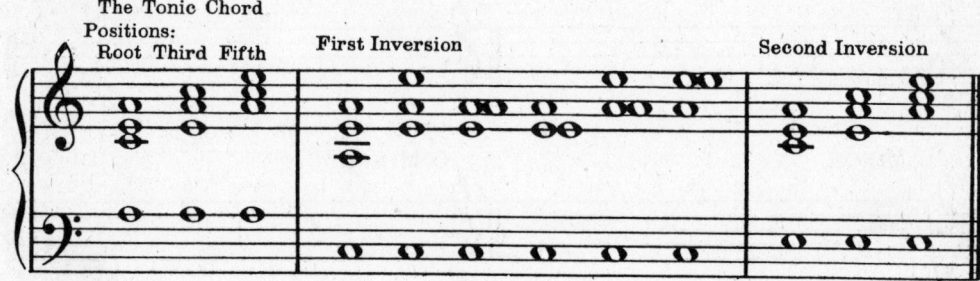

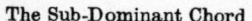

If the Student does not feel sure of these Chords, it would be well for him to practice writing them in various keys with this example as a model. There is no new

USING MINOR HARMONIES

principle involved as yet, **however**. Below is an **Example** for the Student to Analyze. Please write in all the Numerals and Figures correctly.

There is just one addition, in connection with the Figured Bass. Remember, that the **Dominant Chord** is a **Major Chord,** always. Consequently, when it is used in the Minor Key its Third **must** be made into a Major Third (by being raised Chromatically). This is easy enough to remember, however, if the Student will bear in mind, always, that the Third of the Dominant Chord is always the Leading Note of the Scale. This is an important Principle, for which we shall have much use, before very long.

Now as to the Figured Bass: whenever a Sign (♯, ×, ♮) which might indicate a Chromatically Raised Note stands alone over a Bass Note it means, that the Third over said Bass Note should be written as a Major Third; necessarily, with the same Sign (♯, ×, ♮) in front of it. If you have,

for instance, E is the Root of the Major Chord.

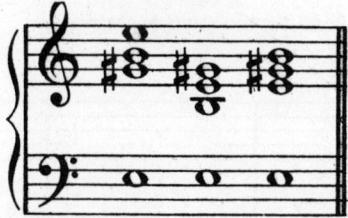

The position to be used is for you to decide: but, do not forget to write in the ♯, or whatever accidental may be needful. If you happen to run into a Dominant $\frac{6}{4}$ (in the Minor Key) the accidental will come after the 6, thus: $\frac{6♯}{4}$

After the above important digression, here is the Example. Please dissect it thoroughly:

Rather doleful, is it not? If we had just a few more Harmonic resources, however, we could make it decidedly spicy. We will have them soon. The Minor Key is not inherently grave, any more than the Major Key is gay. It all depends upon what we do with them.

In this connection, although it may seem to be ahead of our story, there is a matter which it might prove worthwhile to bring up. We are asked so often as to how to tell whether a piece is in the Major or the Minor Key. We have stated, that, in our exercises, we have begun and ended with the Tonic Chord. Nearly every piece of music ends with its Tonic Chord, although it may not always begin with it. Only "freak pieces" fail to conform to this custom. So you have both the Signature and the final Tonic Chord to tell the key of a piece written in the Major. In the Minor, you cannot tell by the Signature, until you have inspected the final Tonic Chord. For instance, no Flats or Sharps would indicate the Signature for C Major; but, if the final Chord were the Tonic of A Minor (Relative Minor) you would then know for certain that you were in A Minor. Moreover, the Tonality, the Harmonies, would tell the tale, in a general way. And finally, the Leading Note, appearing so often, a Chromatically Raised note, would be another almost certain indication.

Now for two Exercises in the Minor: the first a Bass, with Figuring; the second a Melody, with the Student left to his own resources:

USING MINOR HARMONIES

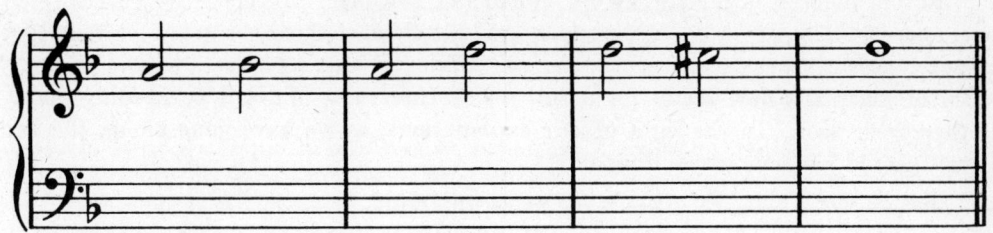

There will be more work in the Minor Key, a little later.

QUIZ No. 20

1. What is the status of the Dominant Chord as applied to Major and Minor Scales?

2. Is the Minor Scale necessarily grave or sad, and the Major Scale gay or lively?

3. Briefly, how can one tell whether a piece of Music is in the Major or Minor Key?

LESSON TWENTY-ONE
ALL THE INTERVALS

The student is now ready for a full set of Intervals. We will be needing many of them very soon. In the light of our explanations, as we have gone along, the Intervals should not now prove difficult.

Here is our Table, with the analysis to follow:

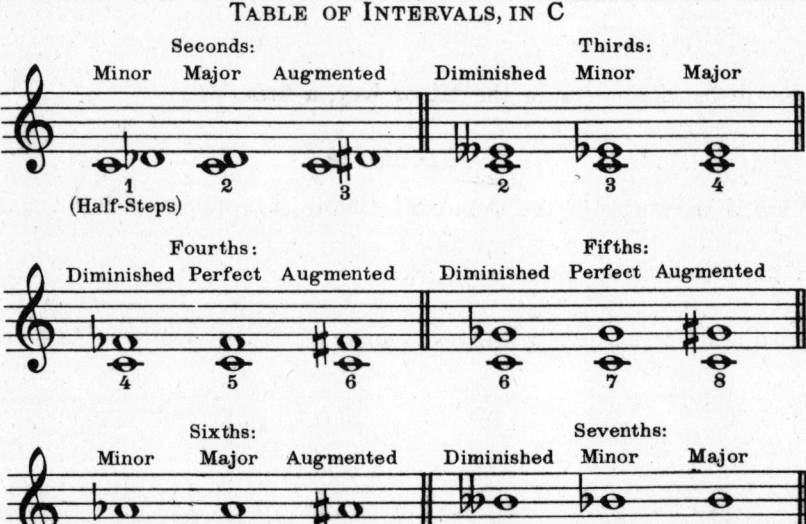

This is a very different proposition from writing only the Intervals to be found in a Major Scale, counting up from its Tonic, in each case. The Diatonic Intervals are easy enough, but these Chromatic Intervals are tricky.

Theoretically, we can Diminish any Minor Interval; Augment any Major Interval. We have not always done so in our Table, however, because we would have created some Intervals for which we would have had no need. As we have said before, the Prime or Unison is not an Interval, not being formed from two Degrees. Hence, our smallest Interval is still the Minor Second (one Half-Step). We could not actually diminish this one, because it would throw us back on the Unison: it would be written, C, D♭♭ (no Half-Step). We have already referred to the Augmented Second, in treating of the Harmonic Minor Scale. How many can sing this Interval, off-hand, with true Intonation? Ah! Better practice it. It was forbidden in Vocal music up to the time of Bach. We have also spoken of those Perfect Fourths and Fifths, either of which may be Diminished or Augmented. We have much use for the Minor and Major Sixth, and for the Augmented Sixth; but none for the Diminished Sixth; so we do not bother with this latter. We have not touched upon Sevenths at all; we have much need for all three: Diminished, Minor, Major; no use writing an Augmented Seventh, since it would take us into the Octave. Now, study them all; write them in various keys; play them; sing them; endeavor to recognize them at sight.

As an Exercise write out this Table, complete in the keys indicated. Watch out for the accidentals! Bear in mind those tricky Half-Steps E-F and B-C! Use the ♯, ×, ♭, ♭♭, respectively, whenever necessary. Do not write Signatures. We want to see just what is done. Here goes:

ALL THE INTERVALS

Table of Intervals

This is something like it!

QUIZ No. 21

1. Name the following Intervals, off-hand:

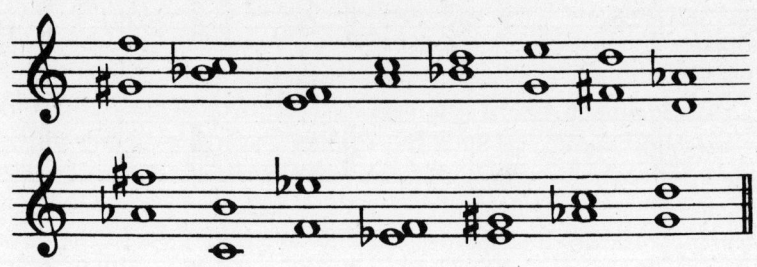

LESSON TWENTY-TWO
BEGINNING THE DOMINANT SEVENTH CHORD

We are beginning the Dominant Seventh Chord rather earlier than it is taken up in some books, but not so early as in others. We believe this to be more practical, as well as convenient. We shall gather up the scattered strands as we go on.

So far the Dominant Chord has consisted of Root, Third, Fifth. More often than not, it has added to it, the **Seventh.** It then becomes a Chord of Four Sounds, and it is known as the **Dominant Seventh Chord;** as such, it may be considered the most important Chord in music. It is indeed well named, Dominant or Ruling. With the Seventh added, this quality becomes intensified. Add the Seventh to the Dominant Chord of C Major, and we have:

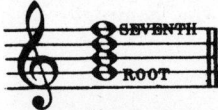

The Seventh is a **Minor** Seventh, according to our Table:

It is known as a **Dissonant Interval.** Such an Interval does not appear to satisfy the ear when standing alone. It requires **Resolution.** By this we mean that it falls upon, or Resolves itself, upon one of the so-called **Consonant Intervals.** These latter stand by themselves and do not require Resolution. They are: the Thirds, Fifths, Sixths and Octaves, with which we have been working so far. Some of the older books do not use the word Dissonant. They speak of Discords. This seems foolish; since, if there is Discord, there can be no music. It was, not so long ago, the custom to insist upon the **Preparation** of a Dissonant Interval. That is to say, the Dissonant was to be heard, in the same voice, in the next preceding Chord, as a Consonant. We dispense with this latter nowadays, although it undoubtedly does make for smoothness.

Here is the Example:

All there is to it: the **Seventh** moves **down,** to the next Degree.

We have already touched upon the tendency of the Leading Note to go to its Tonic; this will cause it to move upward, while the Seventh goes downward, thus:

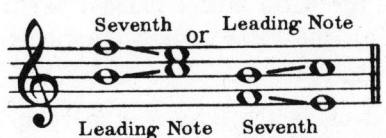

The **Dominant Seventh** Chord, having its **Root** in the **Bass,** may be written in three **Positions**: with its Seventh, Fifth, Third, respectively at the top. These Positions are usually not named:

Although there are other Chords, toward which, from time to time, the Dominant Seventh Chord may move, its chief destination is towards its own Tonic Chord.

With its Root in the Bass, the complete Figuring for the Dominant Seventh Chord will be:

The Numeral (V) indicates that it is the Dominant Chord; the Figure (^{7}) that it is a **Dominant Seventh**: the Position is a matter of choice.

In view of the tendencies of certain members of the Dominant Seventh Chord, adjustments of the other voices are necessary, as the Chord makes what is known as the Progression to its Tonic. The Diagram will show what we mean:

THE PROGRESSION OF THE DOMINANT SEVENTH CHORD TO THE TONIC

At (a), when the Seventh Descends, and the Third Ascends, the Fifth of the Chord is boxed in; so it usually Descends: consequently, in this Position, the Tonic Chord seems rather empty; this cannot be helped. At (b), where the Third Ascends, and the Seventh Descends; the Fifth is free to move in either direction; but our Tonic is still incomplete. At (c), the Fifth usually Descends; the Tonic is still incomplete.

At (a), (b), (c), the Root, in the Bass, may move up a Fourth, or down a Fifth, as may seem best.

For an Exercise, the Student will re-write our Example in all keys, as indicated, putting in, in each case, the correct Signature:

BEGINNING THE DOMINANT SEVENTH CHORD

Play and listen! The Seventh imparts so much character that this Chord should be easy to recognize. We will be using it continually, from now on.

QUIZ No. 22

1. What additional member may be added to the Dominant Chord?
2. What is meant by a Dissonant Interval?
3. What is meant by Preparation of a Dissonant?
4. What is meant by Resolution?
5. What is the tendency of the Leading Note when it appears as the Third in a Dominant Seventh Chord?
6. Describe the movement of the several members of the Dominant Seventh Chord, with its Root in the Bass.
7. Give the complete Figuring for the Dominant Seventh Chord with Root in the Bass.
8. Mention, offhand, to what Keys these Dominants belong:

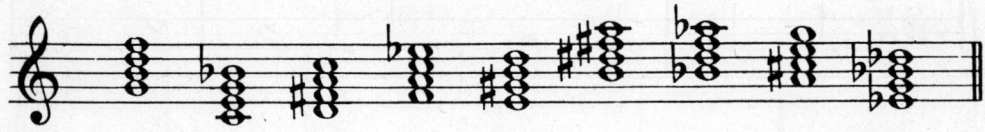

LESSON TWENTY-THREE
MAKING USE OF THE DOMINANT SEVENTH CHORD

We are now ready for some Exercises, introducing the Dominant Seventh Chord. We have just made a substantial addition to our stock in trade. While we are making use of it, we must remember to bring into action all that we have learned previously. It may be that Consecutive Fifths and Octaves may creep in, in spite of us. Watch everything!

We have been following the Second Inversion ($\frac{6}{4}$) of the Tonic Chord by the Dominant Chord; use the Dominant Seventh Chord, instead, if you wish.

Here is our Example:

The student will analyze this for himself. Please mark in all Numerals and Figures.

Now, we will give a Bass, all carefully Figured:

And here is another Bass, less completely Figured:

And one more Bass with no Figures at all:

And a Melody, Figured somewhat:

And another Melody, with no Figures:

All of the above should prove entirely satisfactory. Work upon them until they do. Play them over? Yes, indeed, many times.

QUIZ No. 23

1. As a review, mention in detail all of the Harmonic material so far acquired.
2. What do you consider to be the most important Chord of all?
3. As to their effect, how do First and Second Inversions impress you?
4. Which is the most difficult Inversion to handle?

LESSON TWENTY-FOUR
FURTHER ADVENTURES WITH THE DOMINANT SEVENTH

Much remains to be done with the Dominant Seventh Chord; and much more hinges upon it. We have known teachers to declare that the books did not devote sufficient space to this Chord, and to the manner of its use. We intend to be generous, however, in this volume.

As a matter of fact, except for certain definite closes, or points of repose, the Dominant Seventh Chord is far more effective in any one of its **Inversions**. Either the Third, the Fifth, or the Seventh may be used in the Bass; consequently the Chord has **Three** Inversions. Let us make them all, in C Major, having due regard for the motion of each member of the Chord: The Seventh, we know, always moves down a Degree; the Fifth moves in either direction, but, preferably downward; the Third has a decided tendency to move upward; the Root, in any of the Inversions, stands still. Here is the Table:

INVERSIONS OF THE DOMINANT SEVENTH CHORD IN C MAJOR

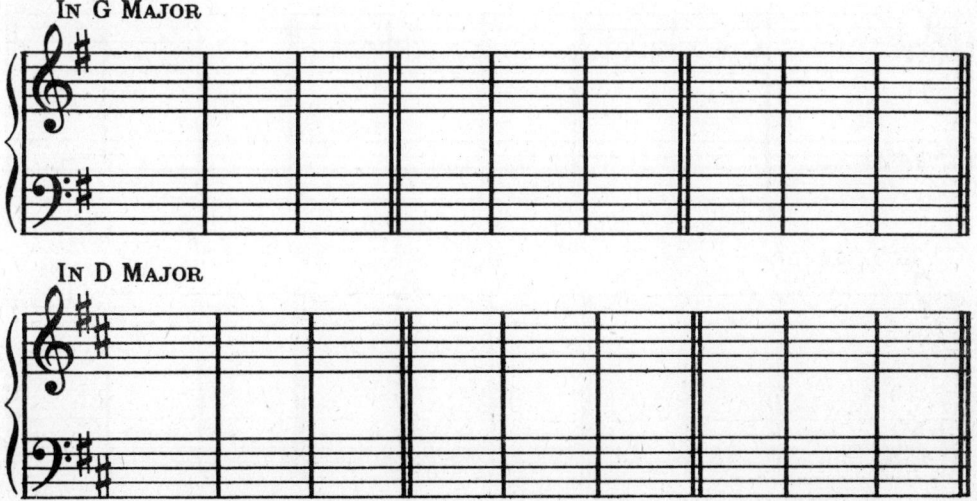

Try these over, again and again. Learn to recognize them, when seen and when heard. Why not try singing them in parts? Nothing serves to render Sight-Singing so secure as knowing what is going on in the other Voices. In Piano playing, one should know any Dominant Seventh (in any Inversion) at a glance; just like an ordinary word. One of the greatest pleasures in music consists in the ability to sing or to play at sight.

There is positively no way out of it. The student must re-write the above Table in all of the keys indicated. Nothing so helps the memory as having to write things down. Here goes:

IN G MAJOR

IN D MAJOR

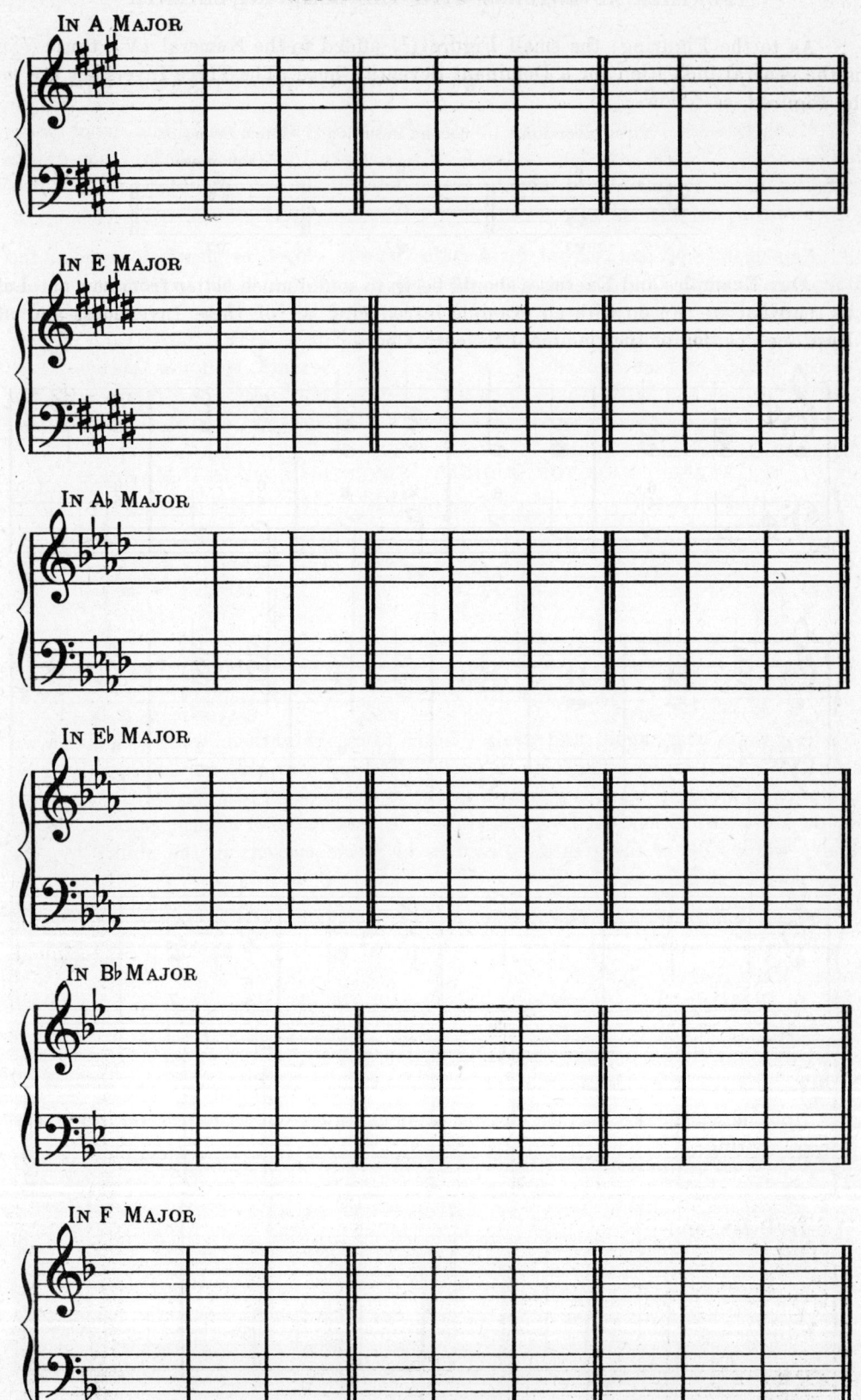

FURTHER ADVENTURES WITH THE DOMINANT SEVENTH

As to the Figuring: the small Figure (⁷) added to the Numeral (V), thus: V⁷; is the general indication for a Dominant Seventh Chord. The Three Inversions are to be Figured, as follows:

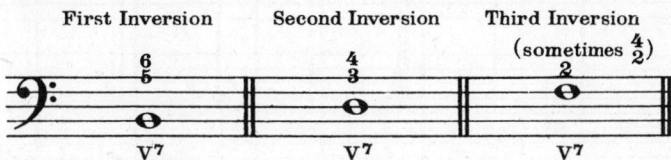

Our Examples and Exercises should begin to sound much better from now on. Let us see what we can do with an example introducing all of these Inversions, and at least one Position of the Dominant Seventh Chord:

And here are two Basses for the student, with opportunities for some very smooth writing:

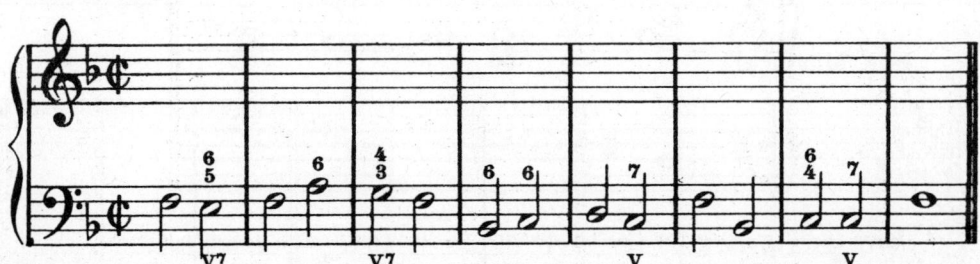

And here is a Bass, Unfigured:

And a Melody, likewise:

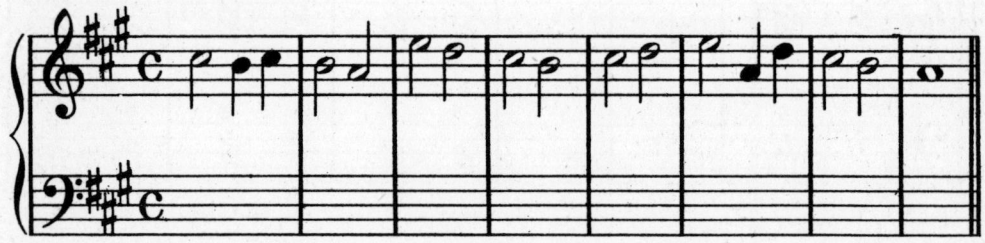

The Unfigured Exercises are each possible of several solutions. Please try them all before writing in this book; fill in the best; then add your own Figures.

QUIZ No. 24

1. How many Inversions has the Dominant Seventh Chord?
2. Describe these Inversions.
3. Name the following Dominants: and their Inversions:

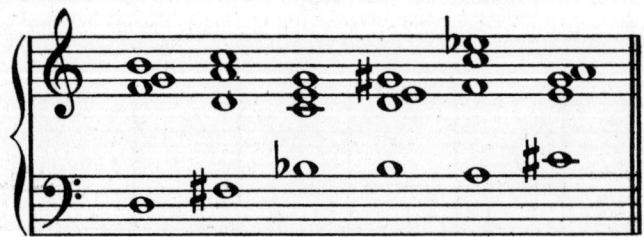

4. Give the Figuring for the Inversions of the Dominant Seventh Chord.

LESSON TWENTY-FIVE
BACK TO THE MINOR

We have stated that the Dominant Seventh Chord is the same, whether the Scale (or Key) is Major or Minor. This fact will be found very convenient as we go along. In this Lesson, we will develop Minor Harmonies somewhat further and also look upon the Dominant Seventh Chords as of the Minor Key.

So far, we may have felt stifled in our Harmonic ambitions, by being limited to just one Key at a time, and to the Harmonies of that one Key. We are now preparing to reach out, just a little further. No worthwhile piece of music, even of the simplest character goes very far, all in one Key. It may borrow Harmonies from a Related Key, or even settle down in a Related Key for a time. We have already explained the Related Keys, and very soon we are going back to them in earnest. Meanwhile, the Minors will engage our attention.

We are accustomed to speak of the Relative Minor, as having the same Signature as the Related Major Scale (or Key). The Major Scale has another connection, which is also very close indeed. The Minor Scale having the **same Tonic** as the Major Scale is known as its **Parallel Minor Scale**. For instance: **C** is the Tonic of C Major, and of C Minor, hence these are known as Parallel Scales, or Keys. Please ponder all this; it is additional knowledge, which is soon coming into play.

We will reiterate, in other words, the statement made at the beginning of this Lesson. One **Dominant** must answer for each pair of **Parallel Keys**, Major and Minor. Here is the way of it:

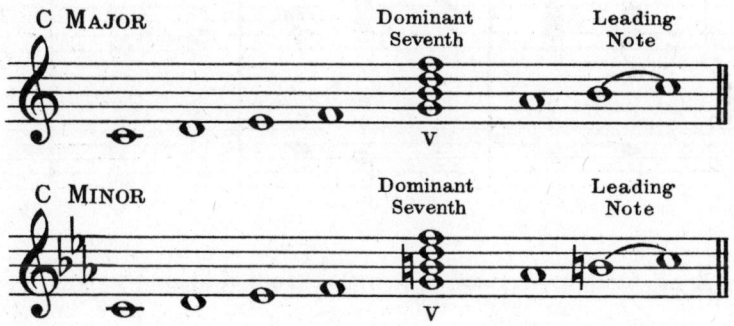

The Dominant is alike, in both cases. In the Minor Key, however, we must remember to supply the Chromatically Raised Leading Note, which is **always** the Third of the Dominant Seventh Chord.

When using the Dominant Seventh Chord in the Minor Key, there are certain points in the Figuring which will require attention: in the Second Inversion of this Chord the Chromatically raised Third of the Chord will be indicated by a ($\cancel{6}$), to be added to the usual ($\frac{4}{3}$) making it in all ($\frac{4}{\cancel{3}}$). The stroke ($\diagup$) through a Figure means that the member indicated by said Figure is to be Raised Chromatically. In the Figuring for the Third Inversion of this Chord ($\frac{4}{2}$, in the Major Key), we stroke the (4), for the same reason, making the Figuring ($\frac{\cancel{4}}{2}$). See Example:

85

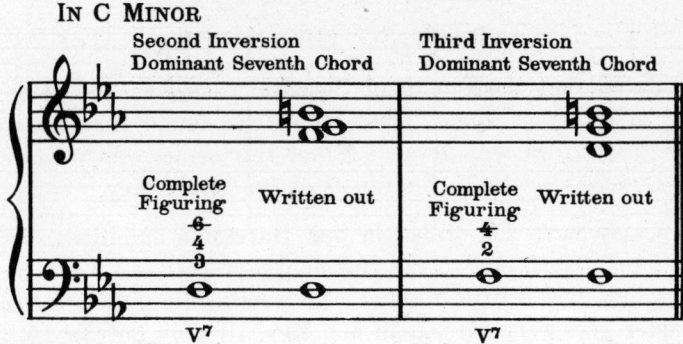

Following is an Example, containing instances of the use of the Dominant Seventh Chord in the Minor Key:

And here is an Unfigured Bass, which the Student should be able to work out handily:

And now, a Melody:

We are still gathering up the strands. There remain a few needful facts, relating to the Minor Key, interesting, and not difficult. Let us take another look at the Minor Scale and its Triads:

I, IV, V, VI, we know all about. But something should be done with II°, III', VII°. It shall be. Now knowing our Intervals so well; and likewise our Numerals: we declare II° to be a Diminished Triad (containing a Minor Third and a Diminished Fifth); III' to be an Augmented Triad (containing a Major Third and an Augmented Fifth); VII° to be a Diminished Triad (containing a Minor Third and a Diminished Fifth).

Now, take:

with its Root Doubled, and in the **Octave Position only**, it may be introduced among Minor Harmonies, if preceded by the Third Position of the Tonic Chord and followed by the First Inversion of the Tonic Chord; or, contrarywise. Or, in other words, we may state, "if introduced by Contrary Motion, between the Outer Parts"

Look!

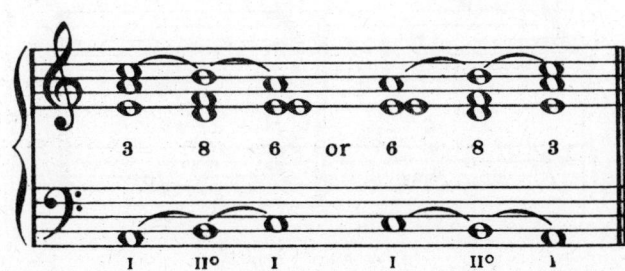

This same Irregular Chord may be introduced in C Major in precisely the same way; but the Figuring will have to be different. Look again!

Some nice distinction here! Where the same Chords are common to two or more Keys, much freedom may ensue. But, look out! We have promised to keep within due bounds.

Next, take the **Mediant Triad** in the **Minor Key**, a Triad beloved of all "Jazz" composers. A telling Triad, sometimes put to ignoble uses. Listen!

As a more or less irregular Four-Part Chord (having a Major Third and an Augmented Fifth), it may be used in **any** Position, or in the **First Inversion**; in the First Inversion, either the Root or the **Third** may be Doubled; the Augmented Fifth must never be doubled. And that **Chromatically Raised Fifth** must always **ascend**. See example, with Figuring:

IN A MINOR

The **Leading Note Chord**, in either the Major or the Minor Key, sounds best, ordinarily, in the **First Inversion**, and with its **Third Doubled**. Example:

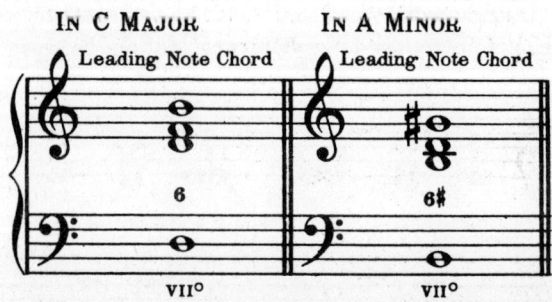

BACK TO THE MINOR

When using this Chord, look out for Consecutive Octaves; they will creep in. Now, pay strict attention to this next Example, Figured where necessary:

And here is a Bass for the Student. Not difficult. No Figures needed:

And a Melody, likewise:

QUIZ No. 25

1. What is the difference between the Relative Minor and the Parallel Minor?
2. What points in the Figuring must we watch when using the Dominant Seventh Chord as applied to the Minor Key?
3. How may we use II° of the Minor Key?
4. How would we locate this Triad in the Relative Major Key?
5. How may we use VII° in either the Major or Minor Key?

And now, let us seek adventure.

LESSON TWENTY-SIX
AN ADVENTURE INTO TONALITY

Those who have expressed a desire for a more extended exposition of the Dominant Seventh Chord will now be gratified, we hope.

So far, we have taken the Dominant Seventh Chord, in its Positions and Inversions, to its own Tonic. We called this a Progression. So it is; but there are other Progressions. We have also demonstrated the fact, that the Dominant Seventh Chord remains the same, whether its Tonic is Major or Minor. Here is another fact, convenient to know, in reference to the Dominant Seventh Chord: the Fifth of this Chord may be omitted and the Root of the Chord Doubled; like this:

IN C MAJOR

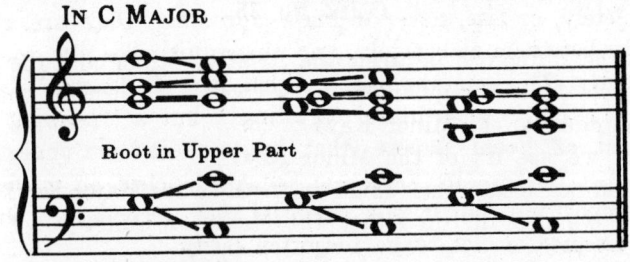

Root in Upper Part

Root in Bass

Take note: that the Root in the Bass moves up a Fourth or down a Fifth. The Doubled Root in the upper Part is stationary. In this form, the Dominant Seventh Chord may be used as taste or convenience may dictate. We appear to be getting very liberal: but wait!

We have stated that the Dominant Seventh Chord has other places to which it may go. It has, indeed. Let us start.

Here is another good Progression: to the **Sub-Mediant Chord.** This Progression is available, however, only when the Root of the Dominant Seventh Chord is in the Bass. This Progression is easy to manage: Simply allow the **Root** of the Dominant to **Ascend one Degree**; and the other voices to move as usual. Thus:

IN C MAJOR
The Dominant Seventh Chord goes to the Sub-Mediant

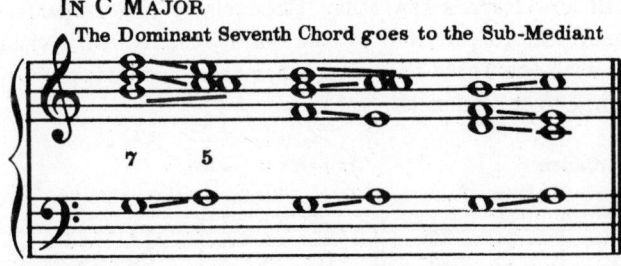

Somewhat startling; but effective, in the right place. It has even more "punch" in the Minor Key. Thus:

IN C MINOR

V   VI

Play these over (Major and Minor), many times. Learn to know them, by sight and sound.

Just at this point, please pardon a digression. We have appeared to stray a bit in this book; but there was method in it, based upon a certain practical experience. For instance: we split up the Intervals, with the hope that they might be better understood and known more thoroughly; not committed to memory parrot-wise. And we are not, even yet, quite through with them. We have darted back and forth, otherwise, for the common good. And, even now, we will take yet another radical step.

Many and many a student has learned the **Cadences**, only, either to forget all about them completely, or else, never to know for what they are really intended. Many of the books list them elaborately, and then quit. We aim to please; but we will try it differently. Did someone ask: "What **is** a Cadence?" Let us tell you. A **Cadence** is a "Falling," not a literal "Falling", but a "Leaning"; such as the seeking of a point of Vocal Repose, that might follow an inflection in speech. There is Cadence in Poetry—in Verse—in Song. Cadence, in music, applies more particularly in composition; but it is so essential that we believe it should be driven home in such a manner as not to be forgotten easily.

Really, the student has been making certain Cadences right along, without actually knowing. We have planned a few for him, in order to make the Exercises as musical as possible, rather than a mere string of meaningless Chords. A Poet is one who "Makes" or "Creates". That is the real meaning of the word. A Composer is a Poet who works in Tones. One of the best definitions of Musical Composition that we know of is: that "it is the Art of avoiding a Perfect Cadence." And what is the result of this avoidance of the Perfect Cadence? Continuity: the ability to go on and on without lagging by the wayside. And what is a **Perfect Cadence**? Just briefly, it is a **Full Stop**. Technically, it consists of the Dominant Chord (or Dominant Seventh, if you wish) followed by the Tonic Chord, each Chord having its Root in the Bass, and the Tonic being in the Octave Position. Yes, indeed, we have been writing it. But we will now learn a few other Cadences. The **Imperfect Cadence** consists of the Dominant Chord followed by the Tonic Chord, with either Chord in its First Inversion, or with the Tonic Chord in other than the Octave Position. Here are the Perfect and Imperfect Cadences:

The above Progressions are, of course, entirely familiar. They are merely taking on a new distinction.

AN ADVENTURE INTO TONALITY

A very Churchly sounding Cadence is the old **Plagal Cadence**: consisting of the Sub-Dominant Chord followed by the Tonic Chord (Roots of both Chords in the Bass).

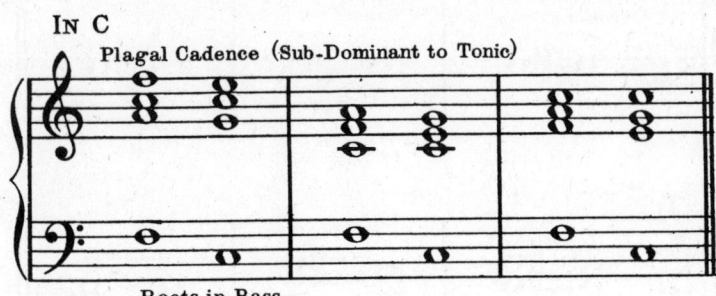

Let us all sing "A-men".

The **Half Cadence** is useful; since it helps to keep things moving: it consists of the Tonic Chord followed by the Dominant Chord (either Chord in any suitable Position or Inversion). Example:

Examples may be multiplied, at will. So long as we come out on a Dominant, we have some place to go, provided we avoid a Perfect Cadence.

On Page 91, in this Lesson we have examples of the Dominant Chord making a Progression to the Sub-Mediant Chord (Major or Minor). This type of Progression is known as a **Deceptive Cadence**: a Cadence wherein the Dominant Chord is followed by any Chord, other than its own Tonic. Naturally, discretion must be employed in managing a Deceptive Cadence; but it is one of the best devices that we can use to avoid the full close established by a Perfect Cadence.

As an example, both of a Deceptive Cadence, and of a very effective Progression of the Dominant Seventh Chord, we will now take the Dominant Seventh Chord (in a Major Key) to the Dominant Seventh Chord of its Relative Minor Key. Here is a beauty:

IN C MAJOR

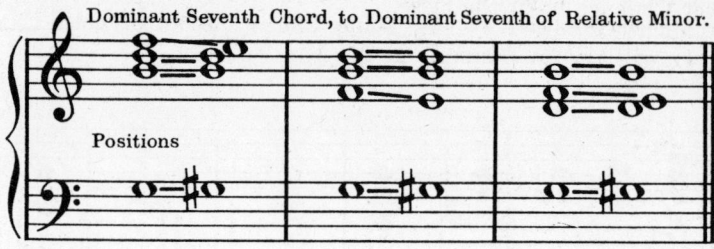

No Figures are necessary at present. It is obvious from our Example, how the various members of the Chord should move. One thing must be noted, however: After we have obtained the Dominant of the Relative Minor, this Dominant, in turn, must go to its own Tonic. In other words: we have slipped out of C Major into A Minor, temporarily: but when we get there, we find the **Tonic Chord of A Minor** to be also the **Sub-Mediant** of C Major. Very neat! Our newer freedom is being established.

It is possible to write very effective Examples and Exercises, illustrative of the fact just disclosed. Let us try an Example:

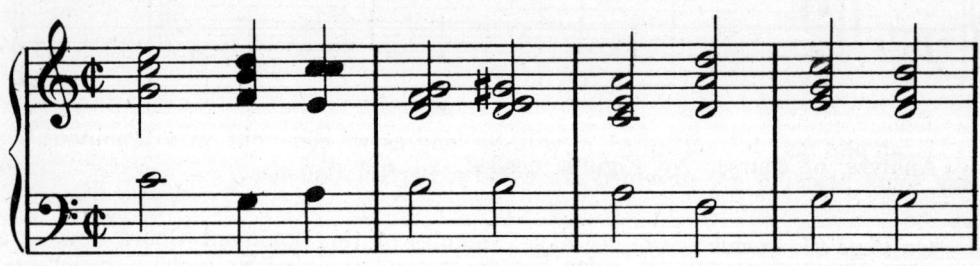

AN ADVENTURE INTO TONALITY

The student will Analyze for himself. Figures are not needed here. There is not a single Perfect Cadence until the close.

And now we will try an Example in the Minor:

Analyze, of course. No Figures needed.

Now, the student will try some Basses, and some Melodies; in both Major and Minor Keys; we will not tell which is which:

Puzzling, in spots, maybe. But give none of them up. All can be worked; and worked satisfactorily.

QUIZ No. 26

1. What member of the Dominant Seventh Chord may be omitted?
2. What member will we double, in the above case?
3. Then, how will the members of the Chord move?
4. Name and describe two additional Progressions of the Dominant Seventh Chord.
5. What is meant by a Cadence?
6. Describe the Cadences listed in this Lesson.

LESSON TWENTY-SEVEN
FURTHER ADVENTURES

Did some one ask: "More Dominants?" Yes, indeed! Let us, in the first place, return to that very interesting subject: The Related Scales or Keys. We are seeking a still larger Tonality, having discovered how easy it is to drop into the Relative Minor, and back again. Let us, once more Tabulate that C Major Scale, with its two Related Major Scales: F and G (see Lesson IV):

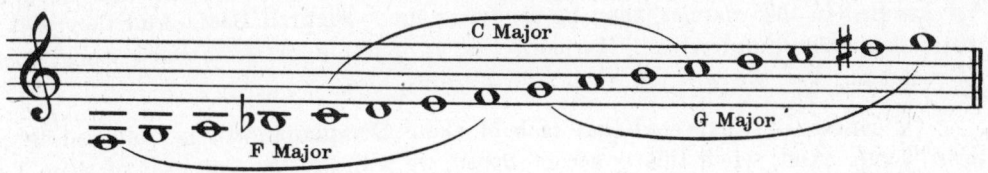

The important truth that we derive from this overlapping of Scales (through the Tetrachords) is the definite Relationship of Keys: the fact that each Major Key has as its **Relatives** the Keys founded upon the **Dominant** and **Sub-Dominant** of the **Principal Key.**

No, we are **not** going to teach **Modulation** in this book. But we can, at least, pave the way. We regard Modulation as a departure into a New Key (either Related or otherwise) and the establishing therein of a New Tonality, for the time being. This we will not do; but, we can at least in a **Transitional** manner touch upon closely Related Keys, through a "borrowing" of Chords, without measurably disturbing the Principal Key or Tonality.

So far, we have our Three Major Related Keys: C, F, G. But C has a Relative Minor, A; F has a Relative Minor too, D; and so has G, E. We will include these in our Group. And then we have: C, F, G—Major Keys: A, D, E—Minor Keys.

And what Chords shall we borrow? The Dominant Chords, of course; because through the use of these we gain our variety. They are the Ruling Chords. Moreover, the **Third** of **each** of these **Dominant Chords** is a **Leading Note**, in each case, to the **Tonic** of one of this Group of Related Keys.

Here they are! Look at them:

See those Leading Notes! They tell the story. There is more than a suspicion, that, when we find a Chromatically Raised Note in an Exercise, it will be the Third of a Dominant Chord and hence, easy to Harmonize.

But, look at that B♭ in the Dominant Seventh Chord of F Major. Again, very easy. The Leading Note of the Principal Key, when Lowered Chromatically, becomes the **Seventh** in the **Dominant Chord** of the **Sub-Dominant** Related Key. Think this over. We have used as few words as possible to tell about it. Whenever you meet a Chromatically Lowered Leading Note, just treat it as a Seventh, for the present, and be done with it. These Chromatically Raised or Lowered Notes are more easily handled in this manner, than by studying out a Figured Bass. And they will be better known and understood. Harmony that is of use, apart from Books and Papers, is real fun. Yes, we will tell about the Figures, also.

Of course, it is expected that **each** of these **Dominants** will be followed by its own Tonic. And, when this is accomplished, we will discover that each of these Tonics is one of the Common Chords in our Principal Key. Just, as we have said before, an enlarged Tonality. Analyze the following, and see:

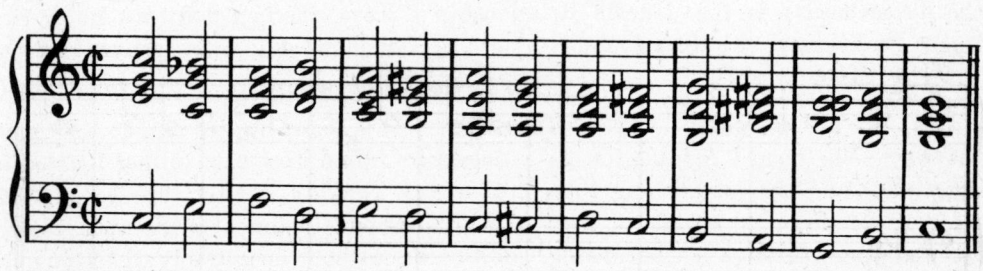

This, of course, is an extreme case. In the space of eight measures we have used all six of the Dominants to be found in the Related Group and, moreover, there is not a single Perfect Cadence, even at the end; besides, not one of these Dominants has its Root in the Bass. This Example needs to be studied. Very likely we would not wish to do this in actual composition; but it is well worth while to acquire the knack.

Now, let the student try a few Basses and Melodies; but, do not seek to force in too many Dominants. Aim rather for smooth writing. It is well to make a Table of Related Keys (with their Leading Notes), for each Exercise:

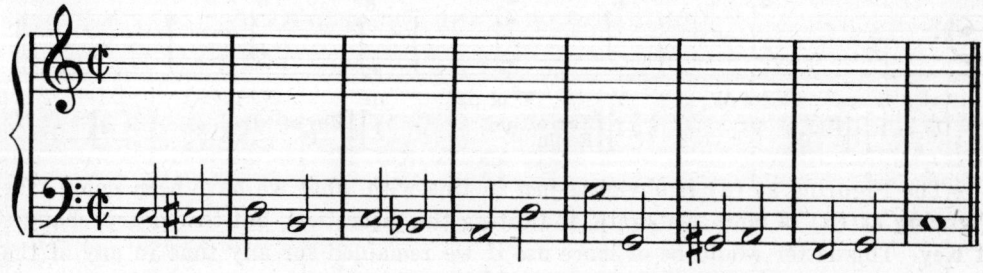

Now, as to the Figuring: take the Bass of our original Example in this Lesson. We will give the Figuring for each of the Dominants as they Progress:

The Figuring at (a) is obvious: just in line with what we have been doing: the Figuring at (b) is more elaborate, indicating the theoretical, but temporary, changes of Key. This latter would be of more use if we remained for any time in any of the Related Keys. Even a Perfect Cadence to a Related Key would hardly count, provided we went right on into something else.

Are any asking for more Dominant Sevenths? Probably not. Let's get on.

QUIZ No. 27

1. What are the two Related Keys of any Major Key?
2. What are the other Related Keys?
3. Name complete the Keys Related to each of the following Principal Keys: G; F; C; D; B♭; A.
4. Write in here the six Dominant Seventh Chords belonging to F and its Related Keys, giving the Progression of each Chord to its Tonic:

5. In Harmonizing, how may we treat a Chromatically Raised Note?
6. How will we treat a Chromatically Lowered Leading Note?
7. How shall we Figure Dominants borrowed from Related Keys?

LESSON TWENTY-EIGHT
ABOUT NINTHS

The **Ninth** may be added to the Dominant Chord:

It is a Dissonant, of course: more so, in fact than the Seventh, which, to our modern ears, seems rather mild. The Ninth has a bite to it. Dissonants are the "seasoning" of Music. In the Major Key, the Ninth is Major; in the Minor Key, it is Minor. We have commented before upon the intimate connection between the Parallel Keys (Major and Minor) and the possible interchange of Chords, one to the other. When we come to the Chord of the Ninth, this is an accomplished fact. The Minor Ninth is used frequently in the Major Key.

It will have been observed that the addition of the Ninth gives us a Five-Voiced Chord; consequently, in our Four-Part Harmony we must omit one Member of the Chord: the Fifth is the best to omit:

This leaves us a workable Four-Part Chord, containing two Dissonant Members: the Seventh and the Ninth. Both of the Dissonant Members must Resolve (Descend). The Third ascends, as in the Dominant Seventh Chord, and the Root moves according to convenience. Here is the way of it, using either the Major or Minor Ninth:

THE DOMINANT NINTH CHORD
Fifth Omitted, Root in Bass

Play and study. In Composition, the "Ninth" is a great "climax" Chord: most effective when used sparingly.

The Ninth should never be used close to the Root, or below it. Why? Try it. and hear how it sounds. Consequently, there are two possible Inversions of the Ninth Chord, with the Root present. Here they are:

INVERSIONS OF THE NINTH CHORD
Fifth omitted, Root Present

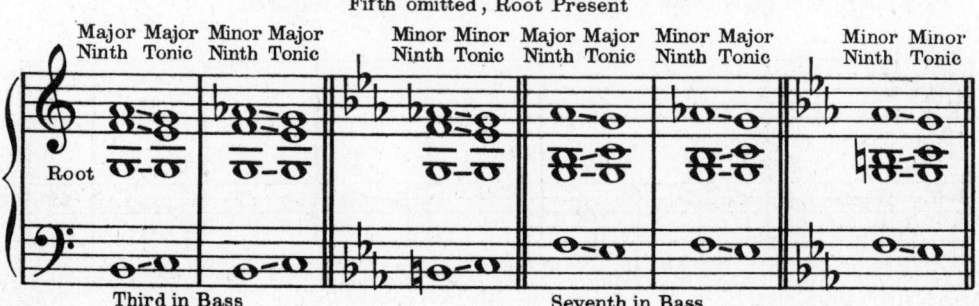

And now for a short example, in which we reserve the right to include any of our materials, previously learned:

Our Harmonies are growing less churchly. We have left space for the Student, in which to write his own Analysis of this Example. Each Chord is lettered:

(a)
(b)
(c)
(d)
(e)
(f)
(g)
(h)
(i)
(j)
(k)
(l)
(m)
(n)
(o)

Figuring? Yes, of course:

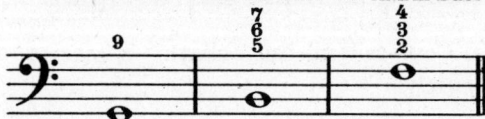

Easy, is it not? Of course, if you borrow a Ninth Chord from a Related Key, you must indicate the Third of this Chord by a ♯ or similar Chromatic Sign, as needed.

Now, here is a good Bass for the Student, all nicely Figured:

ABOUT NINTHS

And a Melody, not Figured. In this one, we would like to have at least two Ninth Chords; and, of course, several Seventh Chords. Try this Exercise many times on a separate sheet of paper, before writing it in:

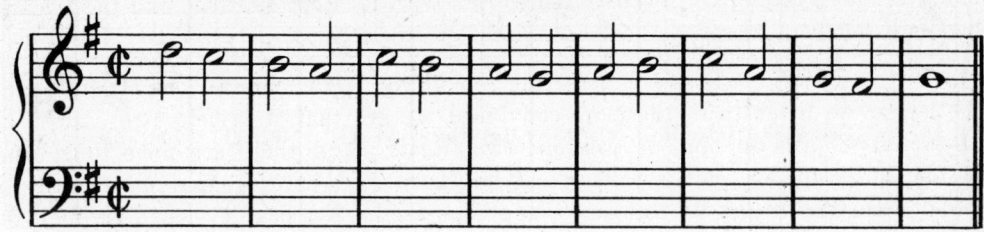

Enough, for this Lesson!

QUIZ No. 28

1. What is the next Dissonant to be added to the Dominant Chord?
2. How many Voices have we now, in the Dominant Chord?
3. What member is best to omit from the Dominant Ninth Chord?
4. Describe the Progression of the Ninth Chord (Root in Bass).
5. How near to the Root may the Ninth be used?
6. Describe the two Inversions of the Ninth Chord (Root present).
7. Give the Figuring for the Ninth Chord.

LESSON TWENTY-NINE
MORE ABOUT NINTHS, AND SOME OTHER MATTERS

The Chord of the Ninth is used more often with its **Root omitted**; and the remaining four Members present.

Yes, we know that we are "starting something". The more we look at Music, and the longer we listen to it, the more convinced we are that it is better to ascribe all Dissonant Chords to one, or possibly two, Roots. And there are none to gainsay us. Music is an Art, not a Science (as has been said before), and our Theory is based upon the usages of the best Composers, as the Art has developed through the years: just as Language, Grammar, Rhetoric, are founded upon the practice of the great writers of the past. We engage in no controversies, but we believe in plain speech and plain teaching. After all is said and done, everything depends upon the manner of "Approach". It is but fair to the Student, however, to explain certain differences. We exploit no fads nor 'isms in this book. Many earnest writers prefer to establish a series of Seventh Chords: one upon each Degree of the Scale, and to wave aside Ninths, Elevenths and Thirteenths (yes, we are going all the way). The disadvantage of this time-honored method is that it makes difficult of explanation certain doings of the great Composers, from Beethoven (and maybe further back) to the present day. As we go on, we shall point out these certain differences; so that the Student may become familiar with both methods of Approach. Fortunately, the Figuring is practically the same in all cases.

To return to our Major Ninth Chord (Root omitted), called by some the Minor Seventh over the Leading Note. This Chord moves somewhat in the manner of a Dominant Seventh Chord, as follows:

MAJOR NINTH CHORD – ROOT OMITTED
Followed by the Tonic Chord

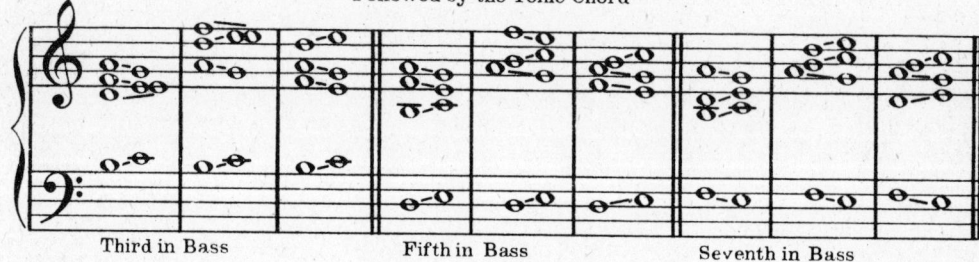

Third in Bass   Fifth in Bass   Seventh in Bass

This is about all there is to it. It will be observed that the Fifth Ascends always; this is to avoid the danger of Consecutive Fifths.

The Figuring is simple, corresponding, in a measure to that of the Dominant Seventh:

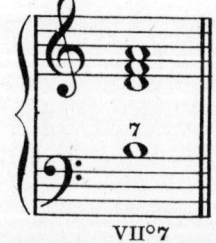

VII°7

with the Inversions indicated as usual. One needs only to watch out for **Chromatics**, when Chords are borrowed from Related Keys.

MORE ABOUT NINTHS, AND SOME OTHER MATTERS

Now let the Student try his hand at writing in the Figuring for this Example:

And now, a Melody for the Student to Harmonize. Use an occasional Ninth:

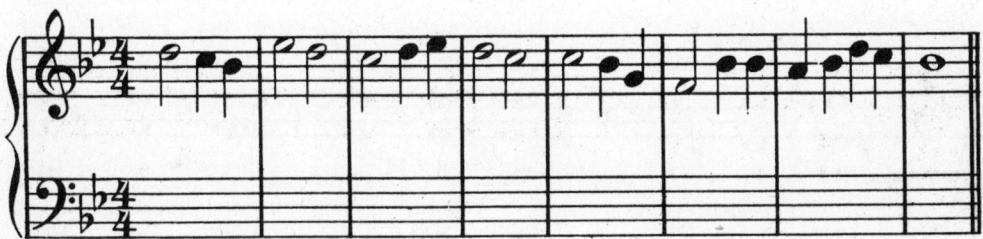

This one may be done in a number of different ways. Write in the book the one you like the best, after many experiments.

So far in these Exercises, we have not been using two Chords consecutively in the same Position; but the Dissonants, that we have begun to employ have resulted in a somewhat freer doubling of certain Members of Chords. So far as the Octave and Fifth Positions are concerned, we must continue our practice as to Consecutives; but two **Third Positions** may be written in Succession, provided the Third in one of these Chords be doubled. The effect is good; and sometimes the employment of this device may get us out of a troublesome place. This is the way of it:

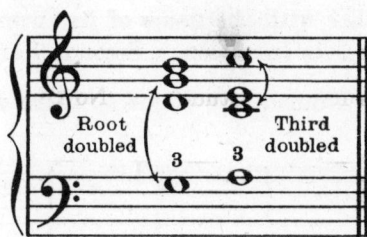

Try this over. Remember to use it, now and then, as may be necessary. By using the Doubled Third in either one of these Chords, we manage to avoid either Consecutive Fifths or Octaves.

Now a word or two more as to the Intervals. We trust that they are all well known and understood by this time. We are just now arriving at a stage where there will be more and more need for a practical acquaintance with them. We will here repeat our Table of Intervals:

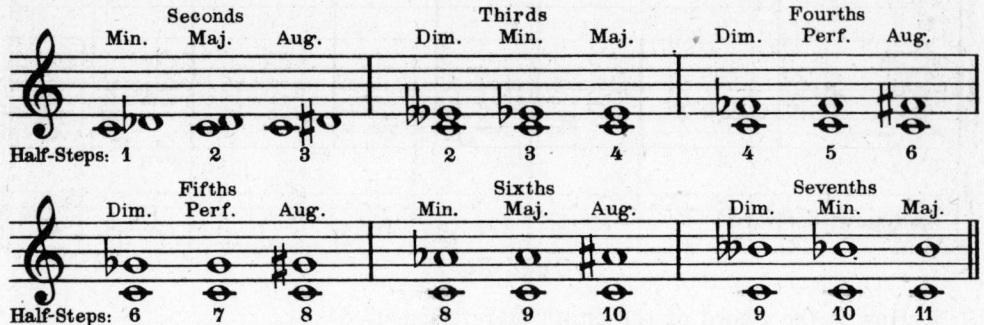

Our reason for doing this is that we are going to **Invert** them this time. Thus:

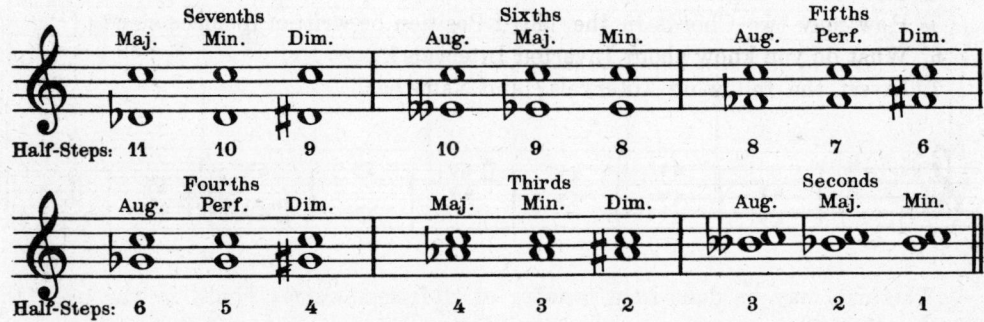

The varied Positions and Inversions of certain Harmonies, and, in fact, of any Chord involving Chromatics, are sure to induce Inverted Intervals. Consequently, we must know these. It will be discovered that the Inversion of a Second produces a Seventh; of a Third, a Sixth; of a Fourth, a Fifth. Note, also, that an Interval and its Inversion, taken together, make an Octave, also, that, since an Octave contains twelve Half-Steps, an Interval and its Inversion will comprise twelve Half-Steps. Another important fact is, that the Inversion of a Major Interval produces a Minor Interval, and the reverse; of an Augmented, a Diminished; but of a Perfect, a Perfect. Study these Tables. We cannot know too much about the Intervals. Note, that the name of an Interval together with the name of its Inversion always add up 9. For instance, take a Seventh and its Inversion, a Second: 7 and 2 make 9.

One more Bass for the Student. No Figures. Make it sound well.

MORE ABOUT NINTHS, AND SOME OTHER MATTERS

And now, forward!

QUIZ No. 29

1. How is the Chord of the Ninth more often used?
2. How else may the Major Ninth Chord (Root omitted) be derived?
3. How do the Voices move in this Chord?
4. How do we Figure it?
5. How may two Chords in the Third Position be written in succession?
6. What do you know about Inverted Intervals?
7. Invert the following Intervals; and Name each:

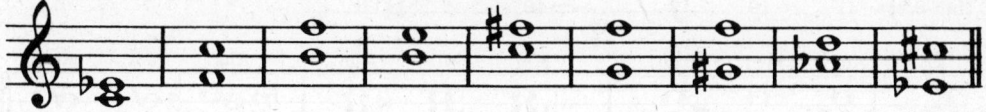

LESSON THIRTY
ABOUT DIMINISHED SEVENTHS

We come now to one of the most important Chords in Music. We have considered the Major, and the Minor Ninth Chord, with the Root present; the Major Ninth Chord, with the Root omitted. We come now to the **Minor Ninth Chord**, Root omitted; or, as it is almost universally named: **The Diminished Seventh Chord**. By many, it is ascribed to the Leading Note, as its Root; and it gets its name from the fact, that, from the Third of the complete Chord (Leading Note) to its Minor Ninth we measure the Interval of a **Diminished Seventh**, thus:

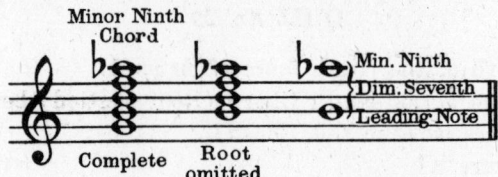

Note particularly, that, starting with the Leading Note, this Chord is built up in **Minor Thirds**:

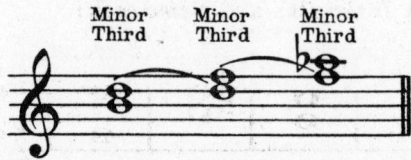

This Chord, although Minor in its characteristics, is Interchangeable; it is as much used in the Major Key as in the Minor Key; maybe more. Although in actual writing, this Chord is given considerable freedom, here is its more usual Progression. It may be used in any Position or in any Inversion. The Minor Ninth (Diminished Seventh) itself in the Bass, however, might make matters awkward; since, it will usually land us on a $^6_4$. The parts move as follows, ordinarily:

The Student should, at once, write out this example, in all keys; for practice and for the purpose of becoming familiar with the Diminished Seventh, wherever met. The Figuring is a little fussy, although not difficult:

ABOUT DIMINISHED SEVENTHS

The Figuring for the Inversions is practically the same in the case of all Seventh Chords, but one must look out for Chromatically Raised and Lowered Notes.

Just as in the Group of Six Related Keys, we borrowed Dominant Sevenths; we can also borrow Diminished Sevenths: thereby greatly enriching our Harmonies. Here are the six Diminished Sevenths belonging to the C Major Group:

Here is an example in which we have made use of all of them:

The Student should analyze this very carefully. Note particularly how closely knit together are the Inner Voices.

In Exercises of this sort, one is very likely to run into what are called **Cross (or False) Relations.** These occur when any Member of one Chord may appear, altered Chromatically, in the following Chord, but in **a different** Voice. For Example:

We must admit, however, that, in the hands of a Master, some Cross Relations may be made very effective.

Just as in the Group of Dominants of Related Keys, Chromatically Raised Notes may be taken to be Leading Notes to the various Keys; and hence assumed to indicate the employment of Diminished Seventh Chords in certain places. It may be gathered from our example, likewise, that Chromatically Lowered Notes may be treated as Minor Ninths (members of Diminished Seventh Chords).

And now for a Figured Bass, for the Student to work out:

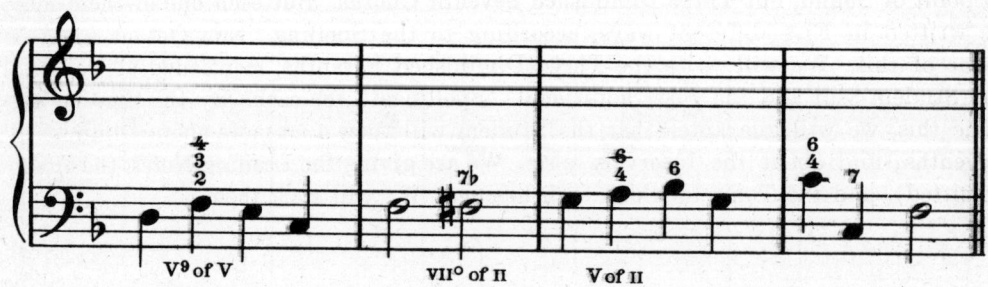

ABOUT DIMINISHED SEVENTHS

This will sound rather gay, if correctly worked out.

It is possible to write a whole Chain of Dominant Sevenths; and also, of Diminished Sevenths. In the case of the Dominant Sevenths, this is the way of it: Lower Chromatically the Third of one Dominant Seventh Chord, and it becomes the Seventh in the next, thus:

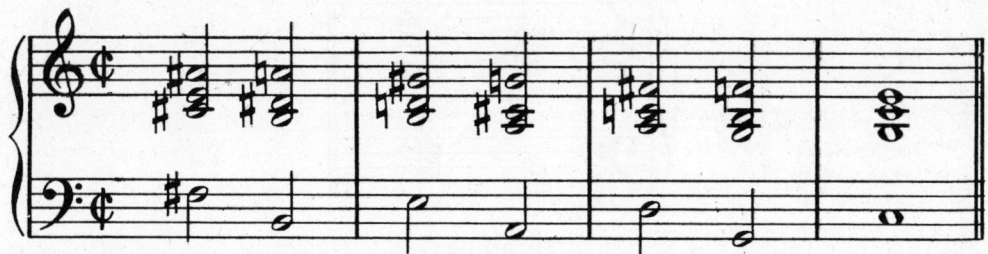

Once more, we are getting dangerously near to Modulation.

This Chromatic Progression becomes still more obvious when applied to Diminished Seventh Chords. Each Member of the Chord descends Chromatically; *but,* the Spelling must be watched:

Leading Notes: A♯   D♯   G♯   C♯   F♯   B
Roots (omitted): F♯   B   E   A   D   G

It's just a Musical trick, after all; too well known to many organists, we fear.

Owing to the manner of their Construction (built up in Minor Thirds), there are, in point of **Sound,** but **Three Diminished Seventh Chords.** But each one of them may be written in Five different ways, according to the Spelling. Now, let us make a game of this. We will write the Three Diminished Sevenths, mentioned above; and the Student will add the Four additional "Spellings", for each. By the time he has done this, we will guarantee that the Student will know a lot more about Diminished Sevenths; and about the Intervals, also. We are giving the Leading Notes, the Roots (omitted), and the Tonic to which each belongs. We will start them:

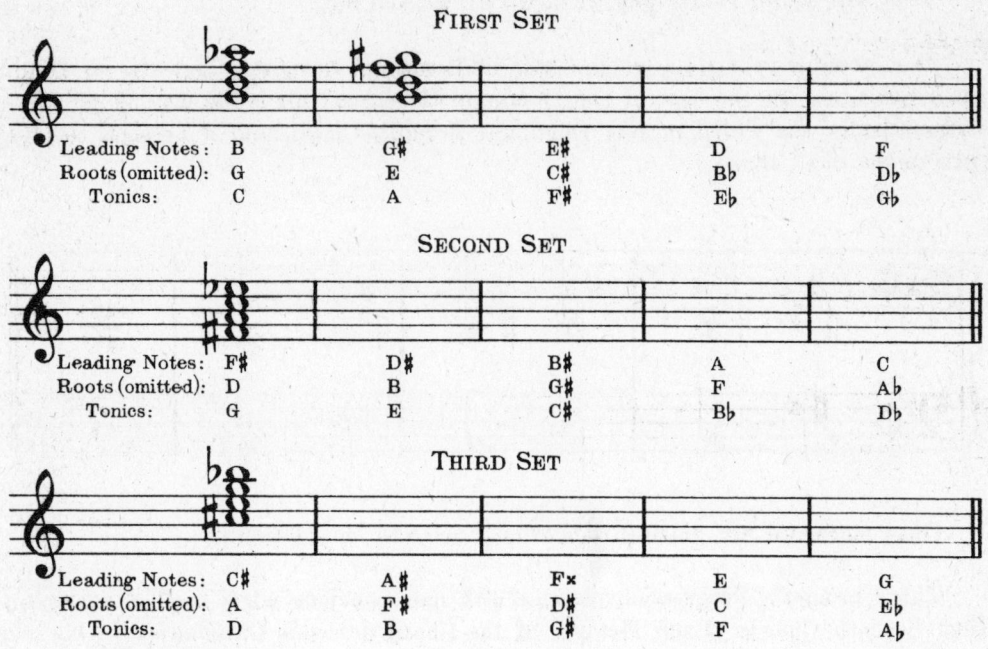

These are Enharmonic changes with a vengeance. Have a little fun trying to pick them out, in printed music.

And now, for a final Melody:

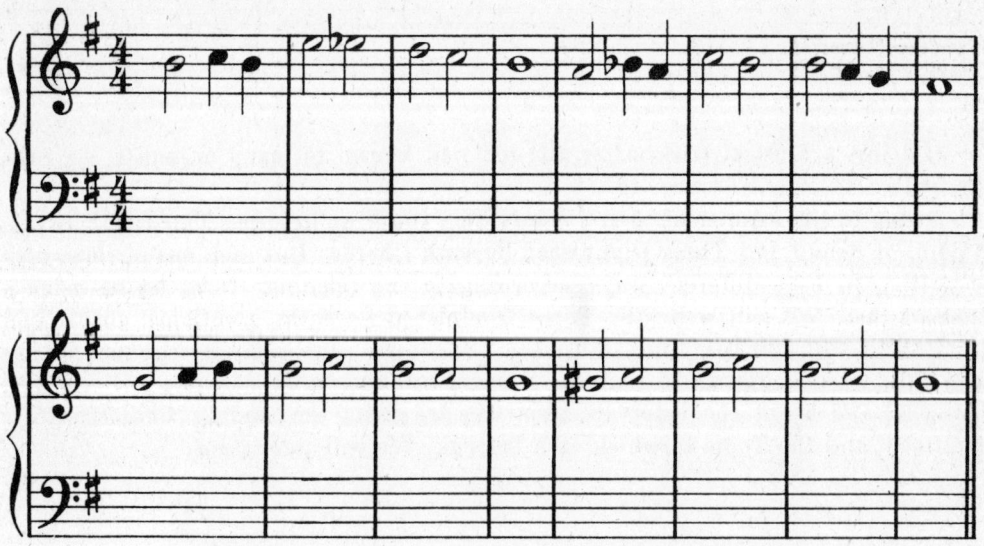

ABOUT DIMINISHED SEVENTHS

QUIZ No. 30

1. What distinctive Name is given to the Minor Ninth Chord (Root omitted).
2. Why?
3. How else could this Chord be derived?
4. What is the peculiarity of its construction?
5. How may this Chord be used, as to Positions and Inversions?
6. What is the Figuring for the Diminished Seventh Chord?
7. What is a Cross Relation?
8. Once more, how may we treat Chromatically Raised Notes?
9. How may we treat Chromatically Lowered Notes?
10. Describe the Chain of Dominant Seventh Chords.
11. How about the Chain of Diminished Sevenths?
12. In point of Sound, how many Diminished Seventh Chords are there?
13. Enharmonically, in how many ways may each be written?

LESSON THIRTY-ONE
ABOUT ELEVENTHS AND THIRTEENTHS

We have always contended that the Student who understood thoroughly how to use the Dominant Seventh Chord need have no trouble with the remaining Dissonant Chords. The Dominant Seventh, and its satellite, the Diminished Seventh, constitute the vital force of the whole Musical structure. They indicate motion, continuous action. The Dominant Seventh, heard so often, has lost much of its character; but, if it be employed as suggested in our Lesson XXVII, it takes on a more significant coloring. It seems valueless to school a Student in just one Key at a time, with just one Dominant. One cannot learn Creative Music in such a manner. Owing to over-use, the Diminished Seventh has become somewhat shop-worn, but the Masters have always known what to do with it. And the rest of us can still learn.

We want the Student of this book to look upon each single Chord of our Examples and Exercises as a "tone mass," considered both individually, and as affected by other tone masses. Sometimes, in the course of an actual Musical composition a single Chord may last for a number of Measures. If it be a Dissonant Harmony, one may hear in its course all sounds from Root to Thirteenth, before the final Resolution. If such be the case, why not talk about them? Indeed, we shall!

Let us add the **Eleventh** to our Dominant Chord, in the Key of C, and see what happens:

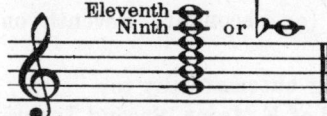

Things are piling up on us: more here than we can use. Yet, many a time, even in a modest Piano piece, we hear the whole series. The **Eleventh** is really a Perfect Fourth, removed an Octave:

The older Theorists treated the Fourth about as they pleased. They called it Perfect, but used it as a Dissonance. What's in a name, after all? The best thing for us to do with this Eleventh Chord is to omit the Root and the Third. In this form, many will call it a Secondary Seventh Chord over the Supertonic: rather long-winded, this latter. It is used with either the Major or the Minor Ninth:

This Group, very frequently, moves merely to another Dominant Group: very likely to the Dominant Seventh, itself. Thus:

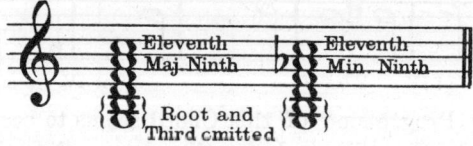

ABOUT ELEVENTHS AND THIRTEENTHS

Very good: all of these, useful and effective, easy to handle; and to remember. We wish that we had had them for some of our more recent Exercises. The Figuring is easy: all Seventh Chords are Figured practically alike; but, of course, one must indicate Chromatically Raised or Lowered Notes. The Secondary Sevenths will follow the usual combinations of Figures. We only use the Figure 9 when the Root of the Chord is present. We use a 4, not 11, to indicate an Eleventh; but only when the Root may be present. In the case of the Numerals, we must use care to indicate correct Keys and Degrees.

And now, for a short Example:

Verily, we are "going places". We will write our own Analysis below. The Chords are lettered:

(a) Tonic, Octave Position,
(b) Chord of the Eleventh (or Secondary Seventh on II), Minor Ninth in Bass; Progressing to:
(c) V⁷, Root in Bass, moving **chromatically** to:
(d) Dominant Seventh Chord of F Major, Second Inversion; going to its own Tonic:
(e) F Major Chord.
(f) Dominant Seventh Chord of G Major, First Inversion; going to its Tonic:
(g) G Major Chord.
(h) C Major Chord, First Inversion.
(i) D Minor Chord, First Inversion.
(j) Dominant Seventh Chord of F Major, Root in Bass, going to:
(k) Diminished Seventh Chord of D Minor, proceeding to:
(l) Tonic of D Minor (Supertonic of C)
(m, n, o) Cadence as usual.

Figure this one? Of course:

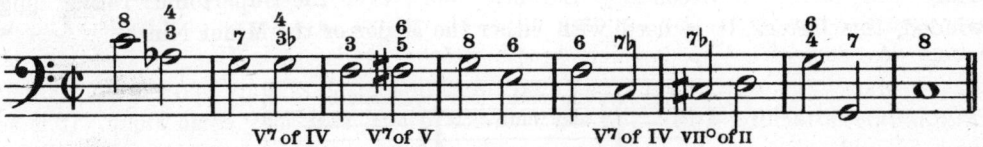

The most effective Progression of this Chord seems to occur when the Eleventh, instead of Resolving, stands still; and the Chord goes directly to the Tonic; more often to the Second Inversion of the Tonic, thus:

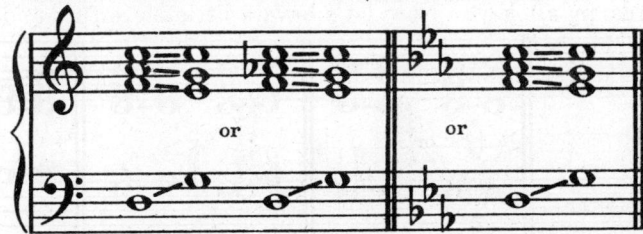

Or, it may be Inverted, thus:

We have called this an Eleventh Chord; and we have explained why it is so often called a Secondary Seventh on the Supertonic; in one certain Position, it is very frequently called the **Added Sixth Chord**. Thus:

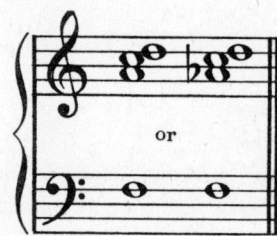

Some very good writers locate the Sub-Dominant as the Root of this Chord, merely adding the Sixth. We see no particular reason for piling up definitions, however; moreover, it spoils our building up of all Chords in a series of Thirds. This is a very free sort of a Chord which "goeth whither it listeth". But the best joke is, that the Jazz expounders have discovered the added Sixth and are using it *ad libitum, ad infinitum,* attaching a Sixth to any common Chord that may come along. It is so much easier, you know, to smack the weaker part of the hand upon two Piano Keys at once.

Just to be serious for a moment; the Student ought to write out for himself, all of these Chords in all keys. Now let's have a little more fun, and build up another big Chord. This is it:

ABOUT ELEVENTHS AND THIRTEENTHS

Yes, the **Thirteenth**; but not "unlucky". We hardly know what some "Mammy Songs" would have done without this Chord (or a portion of it). Music, "what sins are committed in thy name!"

The Chord of the Thirteenth, with the Root present, usually has the Fifth, the Ninth and the Eleventh omitted. It is a Cadence Chord, very satisfactory if not overused:

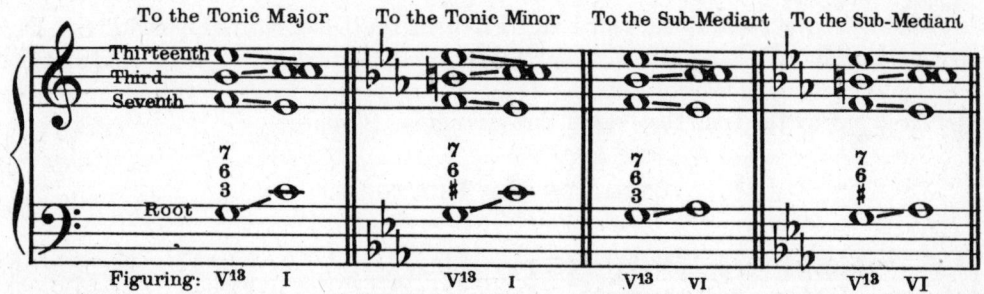

Like any other Dominant, it may go to the Dominant Harmony of the Relative Minor Key:

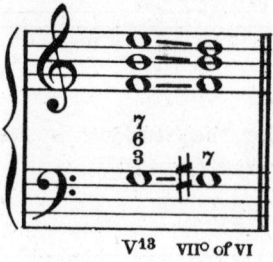

And, now for an Example introducing a variety of Harmonies:

This is for the student's own analysis; but we will call attention to a few chords. At (a) we have the chord of the Thirteenth (belonging to the Key, G Major); it goes to the Submediant chord; at (b) the Dominant Seventh of the Principal Key goes to the Dominant Seventh of its Relative Minor; at (c) we find the Major Ninth chord of the Principal Key (Root omitted); at (d) we find the Dominant Thirteenth of C Major (Sub-Dominant Related Key), going to the Submediant of C; at (e), the Thirteenth, once more, going to the Tonic; at (f), Chord of the Eleventh, with Minor Ninth, going to the Tonic; a finish to the Cadence.

Should we omit the Root, Third and Fifth of the Dominant Thirteenth, we have left another one of those Chords that looks like a Secondary Seventh. This time it **could** be a Secondary Seventh on the Sub-Dominant; but most of the older writers seem tired out by the time they reach this particular Seventh:

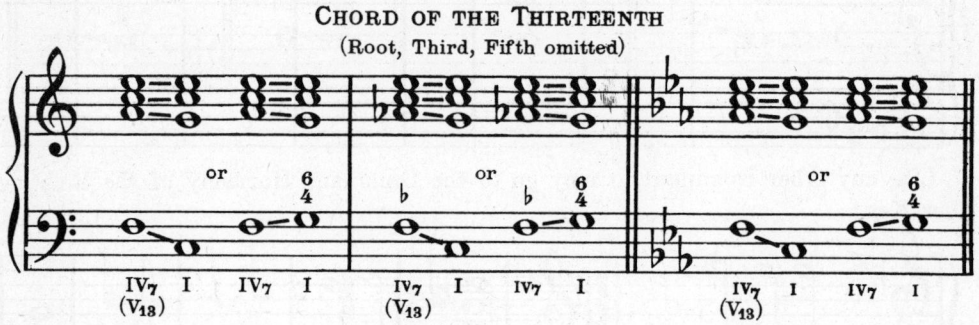

CHORD OF THE THIRTEENTH
(Root, Third, Fifth omitted)

Now, for some Melodies for the Student, in which are offered various opportunities; all of these can be solved effectively:

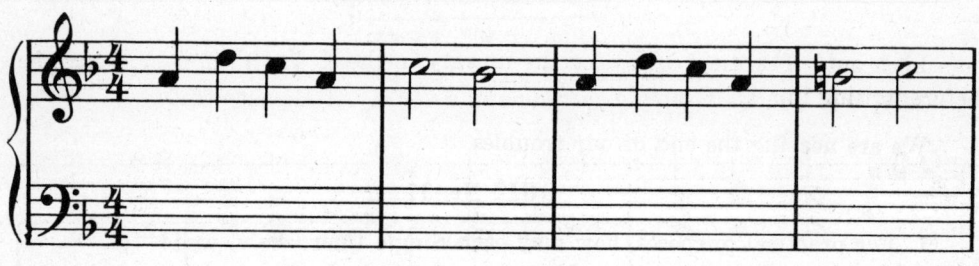

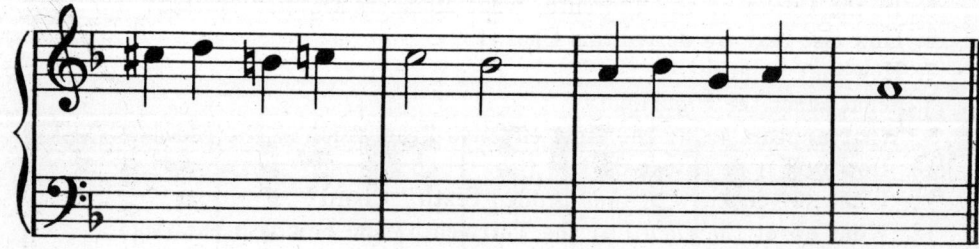

ABOUT ELEVENTHS AND THIRTEENTHS

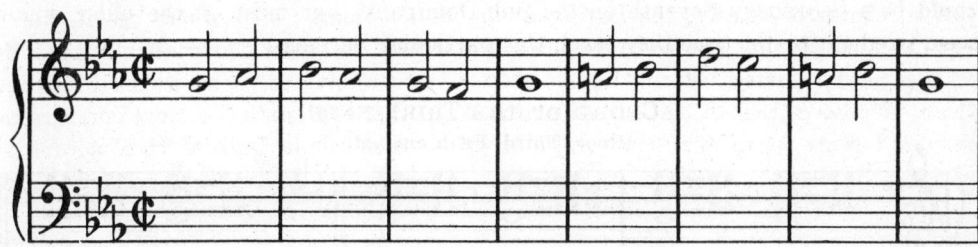

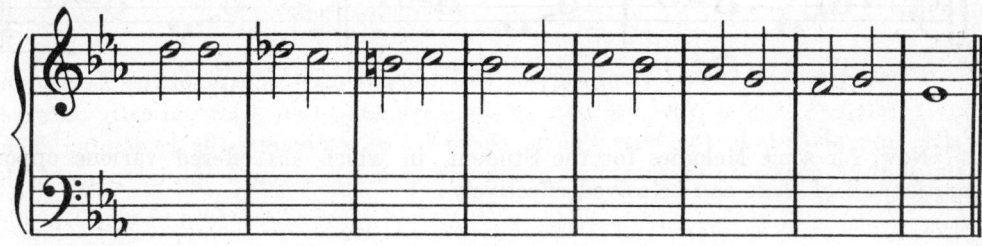

Look out! There are traps for the unwary in these. Try them over, many times, before writing in.

We are nearing the end of our troubles.

QUIZ No. 31

1. For practical purposes, how may each Single Chord be viewed?
2. In Composition, how many Measures may a single Chord cover?
3. Name all the Members of a Dominant Dissonant Harmony, from the Root up.
4. What about the Eleventh?
5. In the Chord of the Eleventh, what Members are best omitted?
6. How else may we derive this Chord?
7. How may it move?
8. What about the Figuring?
9. What appears to be the most effective Progression of the Eleventh Chord?
10. How may it be Inverted?
11. What do you know of the "Added Sixth" Chord?
12. What about the Chord of the Thirteenth; and how is it handled?

LESSON THIRTY-TWO
ABOUT THE AUGMENTED SIXTH, AND SOME OTHER CHORDS

The **Augmented Sixth Chord** is one of the most distinctive of all; it is of prime importance, too. The Theorists are by no means agreed as to its derivation. But, who cares? It sounds just as well. Perhaps the easiest way to locate it, so as to remember it readily, is to think of its **Root** as being on the **Supertonic** of the **Key.** We change the Supertonic Chord to a Major Chord, to which we add the Seventh and the Minor Ninth. This gives us what some call a **Supertonic Harmony.** As we shall see, this latter chord is very useful in itself. Some writers do not mention it; some others call it, characteristically, the Dominant of the Dominant; still others use it, but do not explain. Having reached this point, we proceed to **Lower Chromatically** the **Fifth** of this newly created Chord. Let us show the successive steps as we have outlined them. We have tried to make it all plain. Any other explanation is more cumbersome, besides forcing us to abandon the building of all chords in Thirds. Here goes:

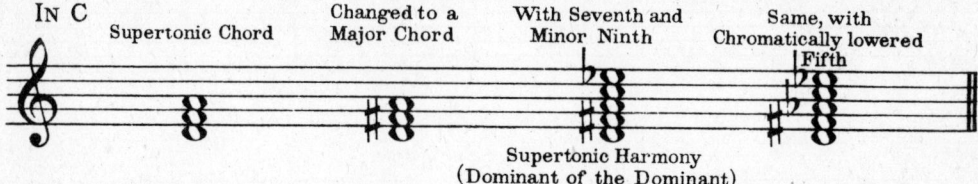

Please read slowly and carefully the entire opening Paragraph of this Lesson and verify—step by step. Now, we can go on. We take that Chromatically Lowered Fifth, and place it in the Bass. Then, above it, we rearrange the remaining Members of the Chord into three groups; each group being given a special name of its own:

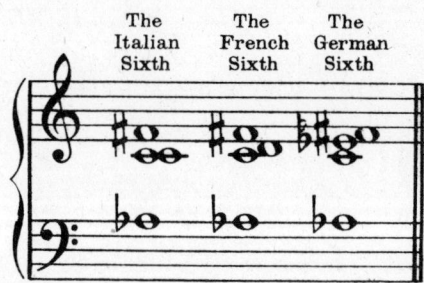

A careful inspection of these picturesque groups will disclose confirmation of our decision to build this Chord up in Thirds; just as we have all the others. Every member of our original Chord will be found, among the three Groups, thus: the Root (D) is in the French Sixth; the Third (F♯) is in all three Groups; the Chromatically Lowered Fifth (A♭) is in the Bass of all three Groups; the Seventh (C) is in all three Groups; the Minor Ninth (E♭) is in the German Sixth. This Chord gets its general Name from the fact that, as ordinarily used, we find, from its Bass to its topmost note, the Interval of an Augmented Sixth. We hope the Student knows his Intervals. As to the origin of the names, Italian, French and German, as applied to the several phases of this Chord: we know not. They are a help to the memory, at any rate.

Progressions and Resolutions? Rather simple: usually to the Tonic Chord, Second Inversion; or, in the case of the Italian and French Sixths, to the Dominant Seventh Chord of the Principal Key. Thus:

ABOUT THE AUGMENTED SIXTH, AND SOME OTHER CHORDS

The Italian Sixth

The French Sixth

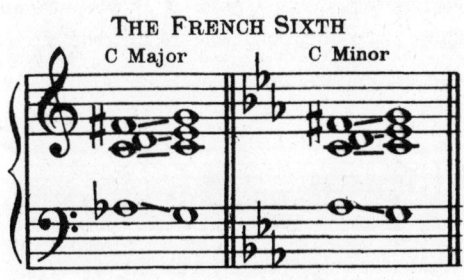

The German Sixth

To the Dominant:—

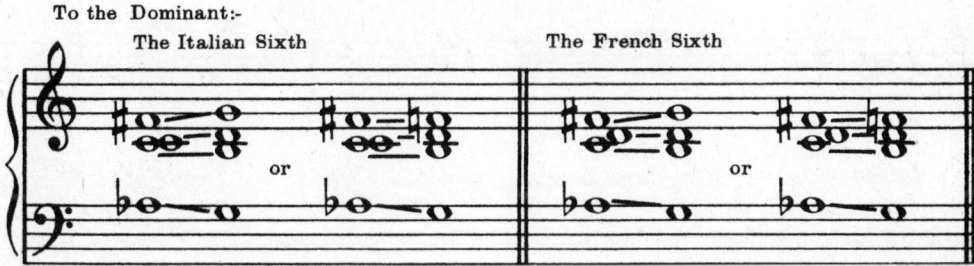

Various Inversions are possible; for instance:

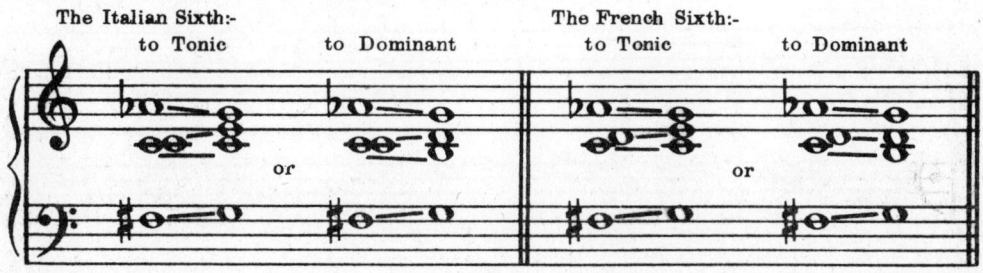

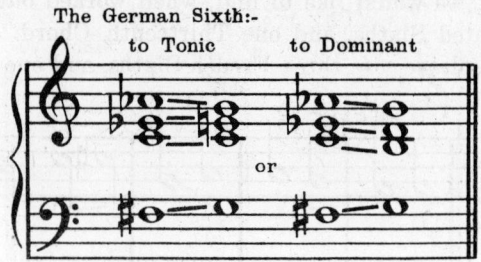

In Figuring the Augmented Sixth Chord it is well to abandon the Roman Numerals; substituting either the abbreviations: It. 6; Fr. 6; Ger. 6; or else: 6+; $\begin{smallmatrix}6+\\4\\3\end{smallmatrix}$; $\begin{smallmatrix}6+\\5\end{smallmatrix}$; respectively, thus:

Now for an Example:

In this example are: three Augmented Sixth Chords; one Diminished Seventh; one Thirteenth Chord; one "Added Sixth". The Student will pick them out; and indicate each one, right on our example. This is like a game; and good practice.

Now, in this Bass, the Student will find all possible opportunities for using Augmented Sixths. Harmonize completely, of course:

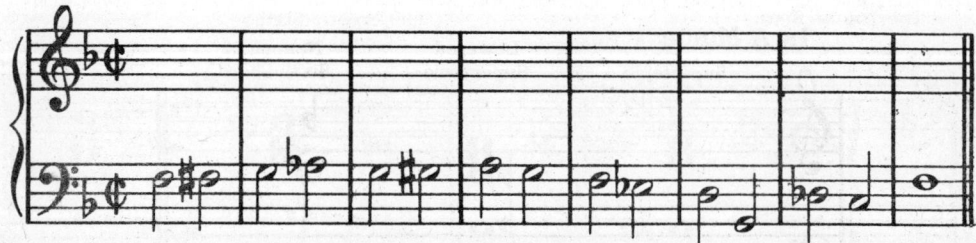

ABOUT THE AUGMENTED SIXTH, AND SOME OTHER CHORDS

In the preceding, we would like to find, when worked out to the Student's satisfaction, four Augmented Sixths, and one Thirteenth Chord. And a short Melody? Yes. In this Melody, please, use three French Sixths, and one Diminished Seventh:

We have referred to a **Supertonic Harmony** (Dominant of the Dominant). We can distinguish it from the ordinary Dominant Group through the fact that its Seventh does not Resolve, but stands still. Its chief use is in the approach to a Cadence. Thus:

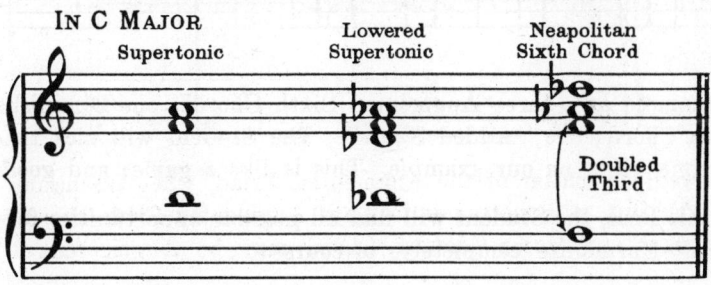

The Chords discussed in this Lesson come under the general classification of **Altered Chords**. It is not a particularly good name, but it will serve.

There is still another Chord deserving of mention in this Class. The **Neapolitan Sixth** Chord. Sounds like Ice Cream, does it not? It's a sweet Chord, too. There is a legend, of no particular consequence, concerning its origin. We obtain this Chord by Chromatically Lowering the Supertonic of any Key (Major or Minor). We write it in the First Inversion, usually, and with its Third doubled. Thus:

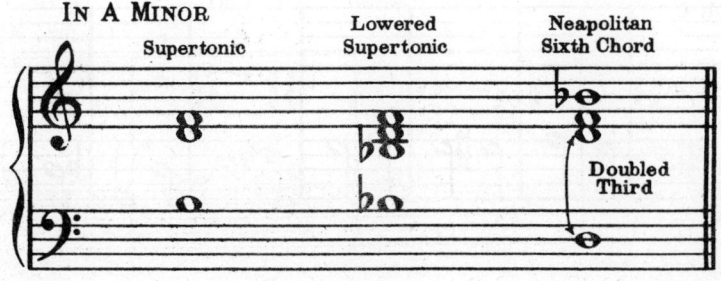

The Figuring for the Neapolitan Sixth (beneath the Bass note) is N.6 or 6♮, instead of a Numeral. To indicate the First Inversion: 6♭. This Chord is usually followed by the Second Inversion of the Tonic; or, less frequently, by the Dominant. Thus:

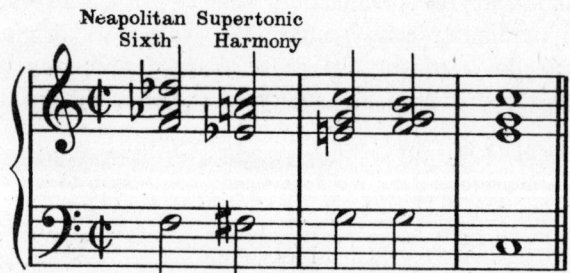

It may be followed, effectively, by a Supertonic Harmony:

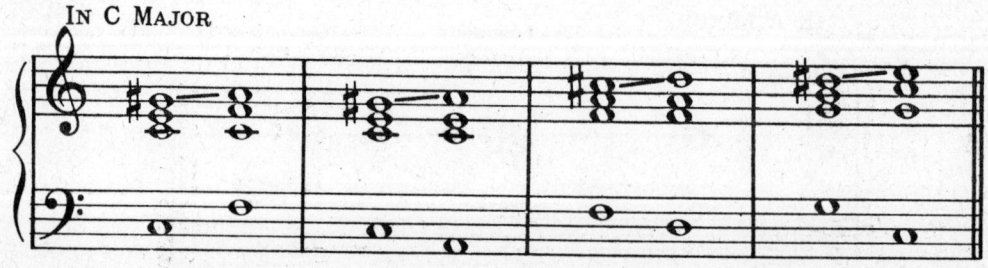

We considered the matter of the Augmented Triad, when discussing the Minor Scale (Lesson 25); but, as a matter of fact, the **Augmented Fifth Chord** is used very freely. The Fifth of any Major Common Chord may be Augmented at any time. Thus:

ABOUT THE AUGMENTED SIXTH, AND SOME OTHER CHORDS

All Positions and Inversions are possible, of course. The Fifth of the Dominant Seventh Chord, even, may be Augmented:

This about completes our list of "Altered Chords".

And now for an Example, containing a little of everything:

There is nothing exceptional here. The Student should be able to Analyze it, very readily, for himself.

Now, an Example in the Minor Key, bearing in mind, that we can still borrow from our Relations:

This may take a little thought; but it is not difficult of Analysis.

And now, some final Exercises for the Student. Basses and Melodies:

Try to discover all that may be accomplished in these.

QUIZ No. 32

1. By what distinctive Name are all of the Chords, treated in this Lesson, known?
2. How do we derive the Augmented Sixth Chord?
3. How many distinct forms has this Chord?
4. How do they differ; and what Name has each?
5. What Progressions has the Augmented Sixth Chord?
6. How do we Figure the Augmented Sixth Chord?
7. What do you know of the Supertonic Harmony?
8. How does this Chord move?
9. Describe the derivation of the Neapolitan Sixth Chord.
10. What about Augmented Fifth Chords?

LESSON THIRTY-THREE

CONCLUDING

Perhaps we have erred in calling this a Lesson, at all. But as the Public Speakers are wont to declaim: "We have a Message". A message and some words of explanation.

We have tried to tell our story, like a real story, with as little of the didactic as possible. We have marshalled our facts in as logical order as possible, and striven to deal with them plainly and clearly, gathering up any scattered strands as we have gone along. Above all, we have endeavored to bear in mind that we have been dealing with an Art.

Harmony is not a collection of Rules and Definitions to be memorized, word for word; or a series of Figured Basses to be "worked out". Harmony is Music: the very Basis of Music; hence it must "sound". We study Tones in their Groupings; and the action and reaction of these Tone Groups, as employed by those best qualified to tell what is good, and what is not: the Great Masters of the past and of the present. There are those who delight in assuring us that the Musical Theorists are at least fifty years behind the times. If this be true, in our case, we are happy in our valetudinarianism.

It has been noticed, probably, that we have omitted all Rules. There is a wise saying: "No Rules, without Exceptions." Very good! If we have not given Rules, we have not been obliged to make any exceptions. You cannot make Rules for an Art; but you can formulate Principles.

In a Student's Harmony, like the present, our lines are pretty well drawn for us. We must allow for such knowledge as the Student already has, and for some slight differences in teaching methods; then go ahead carefully and steadily. We want the Student to know the Chords and how they are used. All else becomes a matter of practice and experience. In this book, we have gone through all of the Chords, but no further. We have, however, endeavored to give a wider view of our subject, by taking into account the fact of Key Relationships; thereby widening our field and enlarging our resources. Without this knowledge one cannot go into the most Elementary Forms of Musical Composition. We have, however, kept away, studiously, from actual Modulation. This branch is better, taken care of by itself. We are apt to get in too deep. But the idea of freedom attained by going back and forth through the Harmonies of Related Keys is priceless.

We have not touched upon such matters as Suspensions, Retardations, and the like, believing these to belong more properly in Advanced Harmony. And, by the way, just where does Advanced Harmony end, and Counterpoint begin? The line seems thinly drawn. To tell the truth, we would like Counterpoint to be taken up much earlier than is usually the case. Oh! did someone ask, what is the difference between Harmony and Counterpoint? We are delighted to tell you. Just briefly, too: Harmony is **vertical**; the Chords are built up, one after the other; Counterpoint is **horizontal**; the parts or voices, though independent, are woven together, like a network. Musical Composition might well be taken up, as soon as the Chords are learned.

The Student may not have become aware of it, but the Harmony that he has learned will enable him to Harmonize completely a Chromatic Scale, ascending and descending, starting from any given Tonic, and keeping within the circle of Relationship of said Tonic. This is well worth working out; but the "Spelling" must be watched. The ability to work in this manner is our ideal of Harmonic knowledge, well attained.

And now, in actual conclusion, we hear a lot about ultra-modern music, and this and that budding composer who, dissatisfied with the Art as it is, is going to show us what's what. Well, we await the issue, in pleased anticipation. But we will say this, that, before any sort of a musical prophet can begin to lead us through his wilderness of queer sounds, he must, first of all, make good in the accepted means of Musical expression, both of the past, and of the present.

Finally, and in theatrical parlance: "Curtain!"